Francis Tibbalds' philosophical approach to the problems facing our towns and cities shows clearly how the individual components that make up the built environment matter less than places as a whole. This informative book suggests the way forward for professionals, decision-makers and all those who care about the future of our urban environment, revealing to the reader a wealth of thriving examples of successful town planning.

Many principles of urban design have stood the test of time and can be applied to making our towns and cities better places in a sensible and economically viable manner. Emphasizing the importance of understanding why some traditional towns and buildings have proved pleasing and successful, Tibbalds argues that these qualities should be built into new developments which are clearly of their own age yet at the same time 'people-friendly'.

Covering the important issues of pedestrian freedom, how to make places clear, easy-to-use and accessible, together with a discussion of building to human scale, Tibbalds suggests that the sought-after quality of 'people-friendliness' can only be achieved through the correct mix of uses and activities. He highlights the need to build developments that will last and adapt, with people controlling the scale and pace of change, and asserts that a clear understanding of how these elements join together is vital to achieving the ideal 'People-Friendly Town'.

This new paperback edition of an established classic includes a Foreword by Terry Farrell and an Afterword by Kevin Murray.

Francis Tibbalds was an architect and town planner with over thirty years' experience in both the private and public sectors until his death in January 1992. He was founding Chairman of the Urban Design Group (1979) and President of the Royal Town Planning Institute (1988)

The ugly American strip or the tight-knit organic European historic town? They are both man-made environments. Yet they lie at opposite ends of a continuum. We need to decide what sort of environments we should be making and how to achieve them.

MAKING PEOPLE-FRIENDLY TOWNS

Improving the public environment in towns and cities

Francis Tibbalds

Francis Tibbalds Le Mans Oct 1988

London and New York

We are all afraid – for our confidence, for the future, for the world. That is the nature of the human imagination. Yet every man, every civilisation, has gone forward because of its engagement with what it has set itself to do. The personal commitment of a man to his skill, the intellectual commitment and the emotional commitment working together as one, has made the Ascent of Man.

J. Bronowski: *The Ascent of Man*

First published 1992 by Longman Group UK, Ltd

First published in paperback 2001
by Spon Press
2 Park Square, Milton Park, Abingdon, Oxon OX14 4RN

Simultaneously published in the USA and Canada
by Spon Press
270 Madison Avenue, New York, NY 10016

Reprinted 2006

Spon Press is an imprint of the Taylor & Francis Group, an informa business

Printed and bound in Great Britain by
Bell & Bain Ltd., Glasgow

British Library Cataloguing in Publication Data
A catalogue record for this book is available from the British Library

Library of Congress Cataloging in Publication Data
A catalog record for this book has been requested

ISBN 10: 0-415-23759-9
ISBN 13: 978-0-415-23759-8

The Francis Tibbalds Trust was set up after his death with the aim of promoting and continuing the work he began. His passionately held views and philosophies continue to be highly regarded in the Urban Design arena. All proceeds from this book will go to the Trust. Further information can be obtained at www.francistibbaldstrust.org.uk or by emailing info@francistibbaldstrust.org.uk.

CONTENTS

ACKNOWLEDGEMENTS

The author records his warm thanks to the following for permission to include in this book, for world-wide publication, selected extracts or quotations from the publications shown:

Jonathan Cape Limited, *The Human Zoo*, by Desmond Morris, 1969.

Design, *A City is not a Tree*, by Christopher Alexander, 1966.

BBC Worldwide, *The Ascent of Man*, by Dr Jacob Bronowski, 1973.

George Melly, article on London, *The Guardian*, 1989.

Rogers, Coleridge and White Limited, *Offbeat England*, by Miles Kington, *The Independent*, 1988.

The Controller, HMSO Publications, *How do you Want to Live*, 1972, *Traffic in Towns*, 1963; *The Report of the Commission on the Third London Airport* and *Planning for Beauty* (by Judy Hillman for the Royal Fine Art Commission), 1990. © Crown copyright.

Random House Inc, and Jonathan Cape Limited (British Commonwealth rights), *The Death and Life of Great American Cities*, by Jane Jacobs, 1961.

All of the illustrations in this book were drawn by the author, with the exception of the two figure ground plans included on pages 10 and 11, which were drawn by the author's younger son, Benedict Tibbalds. All photographs were taken by the author.

PREFACE

In former years, the environment has not been a dominant subject in people's minds. Today it is. We have higher standards. We want more worldly goods and more attractive surroundings. We also want repose. We want to escape from everyday worries and have fun, but not to sit in a traffic jam for hours on the way to the coast. We want better education for our children and job opportunities when they leave school or university. We want to provide for the future, live in the present and keep some reminders of the past. We want roots, we want security, we want to belong. We want to live in a habitat which is convenient, which is human, yet containing elements of beauty which can inspire us and lift our spirit towards ambition and adventure. It is the enterprise and ingenuity of her people which has made Britain great. Now is the moment for us to give our time, our talents, and our individual expertise to help achieve an environment which we can all share, can all enjoy, and of which we can all be justly proud.

That quotation, from a United Kingdom government-sponsored publication entitled *How Do You Want to Live*, was written in 1972. It could have been written yesterday. The aspirations set out therein and the requirements for action are, in the last decade of the twentieth century, if anything, now much more acute. Are we content to let them become even more acute in 20 years time? Or are we going, at last, to try to do something to bring about a substantial improvement to the quality of our urban life?

This book is about the design, maintenance and management of our towns and cities – particularly their central areas. It has been written in the context, not only of a current resurgence of interest in and dismay about buildings and development but also a serious decline in the quality of the public realm.

It has always been easy to identify past mistakes. It is altogether more difficult to prescribe better ways of approaching the problem of making urban areas more *user friendly*. This book aims both to stimulate a new philosophical approach and to propose practical suggestions.

The principal hypotheses are that firstly, overall *places* matter more than individual components of the urban environment, such as buildings, roads and parks; and secondly, that an understanding of what has succeeded in the past can usefully inform the way we design and manage new, innovative environments.

At a practical level, there is no substitute for looking, seeing and learning. It is important to go and look at as many good examples of town making as possible. We can all learn a good deal from principles of urban design and planning which have stood the test of time and can be applied to present day needs in an economically viable manner.

The book draws on some thirty years of practice, observation, case studies and sketching and incorporates some of the themes developed during an enjoyable year as President of the Royal Town Planning Institute in 1988.

I do not want it to be an opaque or esoteric book. It is addressed to a wide range of professionals, students and interested lay people both in the United Kingdom and internationally and I hope that its messages are useful, clear and simple.

I should like to dedicate this book to a number of people who have all genuinely influenced my thinking on the matters covered herein. They are Walter Bor, the late Dr Jacob Bronowski, Sir Colin Buchanan, Jonathon Porritt, Jaquelin Robertson and His Royal Highness The Prince of Wales. Coupled with these names I would like to record warmest thanks to my wife, Janet, and two sons, Adam and Benedict, who supported this endeavour and quietly suffered me sitting at a word processor and sketch pad for hours on end. Warm thanks must also go to Maritz Vandenberg for encouraging me to write the book in the first place and maintaining a fatherly interest in its progress. Finally, I must also humbly acknowledge the many hundreds of people simply going about their business in different parts of the world, whom I have observed and listened to as they enjoy – or loathe – their local physical environment.

Foreword

I first met met Francis Tibbalds during the 1980s in connection with the Urban Design Group. One of his singular achievements was bringing urban design to the general attention of architects, planners, landscape architects and even politicians. The founding of the Urban Design Group in 1979 was quite a milestone and led to the subsequent awareness of urban design in Britain. The group was led by far-sighted and passionate people as well as Francis – John Worthington of DEGW, Jane Priestman and Alan Baxter, among others. These people not only saw urban design as the way forward and the answer to much of the country's urban problems but were also able to offer an insight into the nature of these problems.

Francis' outlook towards urban design was one with which I have great sympathy. His deep interest in urbanism extended to an understanding of how the city works as a historical layering of successive generations – the city as the work of many hands. The best solutions to the city's problems arise from a collaboration of different professionals and under Francis' leadership various multi-disciplinary people were brought together. The Urban Design Group exemplified this 'many hands' approach as planners, architects and other environmentalists worked together to create environments that responded to people's needs. In 1988 he brought out his award-winning 'Ten Commandments of Good Urban Design', where his statements – 'Thou shalt consider places before buildings'; 'Thou shalt have the humility to learn from the past and respect thy context' – now seem so obvious but were then quite controversial. Looking beyond the confines of design, as President of the Royal Town Planning Institute, Francis lobbied for political action toward homelessness as well as the improvement of public transport infrastructure.

He would be extremely pleased to see how the debate has been widened today, particularly through the Urban Design Alliance (UDAL), which has extended the thinking and concepts behind the Urban Design Group and transformed it into a broad-based, professional group of architects, civil engineers, town planners, surveyors and landscape architects. UDAL works alongside the Urban Design Group, and is now recognised as one of the strong forces speaking for urban design. I am sure Francis would marvel at the results of the govenment-backed Urban Task Force and its report *Towards an Urban Renaissance*, and especially the way politicians and ministers of state so frequently use the very words 'urban design' as part of their accepted language. Equally pronounced is the revolution towards urbanism in the field of design. Every architect and designer recognises that the future of our cities is a central theme. This outlook is in marked contrast to the time in which Francis and his colleagues launched the Urban Design Group.

As well as collaborating together on the Urban Design Group, Francis and I overlapped professionally. His practice, Tibbalds Monro, worked with TFP very successfully on many projects. Francis had a wonderful skill with drawings, as well as great clarity of thinking in terms of understanding problems and expressing solutions. He set up an extremely good practice with very sound, gifted people around him. We enjoyed working together on the development at King's Cross, for example, where our alternative scheme – low-rise, public transport-based and not grandiose – was one of the serious contenders to unravel the problems and missed opportunities of that area in the 1980s. We also collaborated on a scheme for a shopping complex in Wimbledon Town Centre. This project was a good example of thinking in urban-design terms in that it produced alternatives to the common anti-urban solutions. He and I were consequently often pitched together against the forces of ignorance and grandiose modernity that then characterised urban planning. Finally, we collaborated on the redevelopment of Charing Cross station and masterplan. This was one I remember best because we worked together not only as urban designers on the area around the station, but also on detailed design and cladding.

I remember Francis as extraordinarily professional, very earnest and hardworking, with a passion and commitment to his work and the field he worked in. This is exemplified by the reputation of his practice and also of course his professional roles – he was President of the Royal Town Planning Institute and Vice President of the European Council of Town Planners. But for me his lasting memory is his contribution as a draftsman and artist. Not only are his sketches wonderfully good, but he also had the ability to do simple diagrams that encapsulated his whole wider thought in an extraordinarily simple way. In particular, Francis was a great asset to London, tirelessly championing its heritage and improvement. In general, he elevated urban design from a minority interest into a cause at the forefront of urban thinking.

Making People-Friendly Towns is a fitting epitaph to what Francis thought, what he stood for, what he achieved and how he presented his work. The book is as relevant today as it was when he completed it, just days before he died.

Terry Farrell
March 2000

Francis Tibbalds Birmingham 1989/90

1

The Decline of the Public Realm

We have reached a stage in the development of our technology where we have the power to create the environment we need or to destroy it beyond repair, according to the use we make of our power. This forces us to control this power. To do this, we must first of all decide what we want to achieve. And this is far from easy....

Sir Ove Arup: *How Do You Want to Live?*

The need to care about the urban environment has never been greater. Towns and cities over the centuries must surely rank as the greatest achievements of technological, artistic, cultural and social endeavour. The *public realm* is, in my view, the most important part of our towns and cities. It is where the greatest amount of human contact and interaction takes place. It is all the parts of the urban fabric to which the public have physical and visual access. Thus, it extends from the streets, parks and squares of a town or city into the buildings which enclose and line them.

I want to suggest, however, that the public realm in many countries is under threat and never more so than in the last decade. Great Britain, for example, used to be acclaimed for leading the world in civilized urban living – in transport, housing, health and culture. It had a very rich public domain.

Yet we are now witnessing a serious decline of this rich domain. Many of the world's towns and cities – especially their centres – have become threatening places – littered, piled with rotting rubbish, covered in graffiti, polluted, congested and choked by traffic, full of mediocre and ugly poorly main-

tained buildings, unsafe, populated at night by homeless people living in cardboard boxes, doorways and subways and during the day by many of the same people begging on the streets. Developers and owners gate their developments. They exclude the public from shopping centre malls and street level office atria at evenings and weekends. Most new buildings do not say '*Come in...welcome*', they say '*Sod off...go away!*'. Buildings and cities, have, to many, become little more than vehicles for making money. It needs to be recognized that the simple pursuit of profit and economic growth is not usually compatible with improving the quality of our urban life-style.

At the same time that the *public* realm has declined there has been a corresponding flourishing of the *private* realm – with an emphasis on privacy, retreat, personal comfort, private consumption and security. Looking after 'me first', in a rather nasty thing called the 'enterprise culture'. The public realm is an SEP (for those unfamiliar with Douglas Adams – *someone else's problem*).

One sees this selfish attitude epitomized nowhere more cogently than at the now crudely gated

It does not matter where this actually is. It exemplifies a city centre which underwent rapid change in the 1950s and 1960s in terms of unprecedented built development and highway construction. It offers a physical environment which now falls far short of current public aspirations.

Similarly, it does not matter where the photographs used to illustrate this chapter are taken from. Collectively, they illustrate the decline and neglect of the public environment which is taking place in many towns and cities around the world, largely as a result of poverty of imagination, lack of caring and under-investment of resources.

Many private developments are now gated. Towns and cities are losing their identity and becoming drab traffic-oriented, tower-block dominated places that are the same all over the world.

entrance to Downing Street. Under our very noses, the former British Prime Minister got away with privatizing one of the most famous streets in the world! And in many places private house developers are following this appalling example and gating their developments to make exclusive, protected enclaves.

Against this dreadful background, public interest in and concern about the built environment has never been greater. In Britain this is partly as a result of the outspoken views of His Royal Highness The Prince of Wales. And, it would appear, the problems of London and Britain can be found in many towns and cities around the world – including those in North America, Europe and Australasia.

Taking an overview of urban areas can certainly be a depressing experience. In many cities, particularly European ones, the centres are characterized by an appealing maze-like, intricate quality, in which sit – sometimes comfortably, at other times less so – one-off edifices left by Church, State, industry or commerce. The peripheries are usually typified by rather dull and soul-less residential suburbs. Inner areas display bleak, decaying blocks of flats

and slum properties. The whole urban area is beset by dirty, noisy traffic congestion and quite probably is cut through with crude urban motorways, which have had a devastating impact on the local environments through which they pass. The better endowed towns and cities in Europe have received the benefit of considerable investment in their heritage, making them ever more attractive to tourists and a mono-culture of hotels, restaurants, cafés, chic shops, and various themed experiences – a sort of ubiquitous Disneyland.

Four-fifths of Europeans live in towns and cities. Car ownership is rising. Places are losing their individuality. It is all too easy for a city to destroy its heritage and lose what is unique to it, in favour of a car-oriented, tower-block dominated place that can be seen anywhere in the world. Urban areas are sprawling and land uses are separated in a manner that makes the provision of transport facilities difficult and expensive. Some cities are even without proper government.

New development is often bland and mediocre. Cynicism at the plight of our cities was succinctly caricatured by Miles Kington, writing in *The*

Independent in July 1988 and explaining Offbeat England to tourists:

'Is a city a town with a cathedral?'
'No. A city is a town with a high-rise car park blotting out the view of the cathedral. Other features of a city include a branch of Laura Ashley, a twinning operation with more than one foreign town, a railway station inconveniently far from the centre, a local evening paper which hasn't sold out by 3pm, a football team which hopes to get back into the First Division, a local radio station playing the same American records as everyone else, branches of all the main clearing banks plus one other, at least two concrete overpasses, a taxi rank with more than five cabs waiting and a ring road. On the ring road you will see signs to the City Centre. If you follow these, you will eventually end up in a cul-de-sac behind the cinema. Nobody knows why'.

I'm sure readers will recognize it!

The sobering fact of the matter is that most urban areas have become a mess, they are not *people-friendly* and over the past few decades, albeit with the best intentions, we have only succeeded in making the situation incomparably worse. We need a fresh look at what really matters to people who use urban areas. We need to look at urban areas as a whole and not as a series of unrelated, but competing, sectoral interests. Most of all we need the commitment of the inhabitants and users of cities and towns. They must be interested not just in creating commercial viability, tourist attractions, livability, sustainability, greenness or any of a dozen, trendy epithets now being applied to urban areas, but they must shout loudly *'we want a better quality of life for the city as a whole'* and commit to achieving this.

So how can we improve the design and maintenance of a public realm which is currently so starved of imagination and resources?

The thrust of the book is simple and non-negotiable: The achievement of *good design* must be a fundamental objective of the planning system and development industry. I am broad-minded about how this might be achieved.

Urban designers deal in dreams, or visions. They need all sorts of tricks up their sleeves to implement those visions or to persuade others that they are worth implementing. Codes and Rule Books can be part of the tools of trade of the urban designer, but only part. We must be careful not to make everything too prescriptive – too neat and tidy. Urban areas are messy and complex, rich and muddled. The process of urban design needs

Shops and shopping have had a particularly devastating impact on many towns and cities – from the banal fascias and huge, bland glazed display areas which bear little relationship to the building in which they are set, to the ubiquitous indoor shopping mall, out of town centre and one-off cash and carry facility – all of which exhibit generally mediocre standards of design.

to leave room for messiness and complexity! Sir Paul Reilly asserted:

There is in all city dwellers a built-in requirement for the three H's – higgledy-piggledy, hugger-mugger and hulla-baloo. Anyone walking round the new city centre of Plymouth at nine o'clock at night will appreciate the gloomy absence of these qualities.

My starting point is that design is not something rather superficial, added when everything else is decided. The dreadful phrase *aesthetic control* does, I'm afraid, conjure up exactly the wrong impression. I am sure that readers will know the story about the aftermath of a hurricane in the United States. An anxious chairman of a major retailing development company called the manager of a shopping centre which lay right in the hurricane's path to enquire what the damage had been. 'The buildings are fine' he was told, 'but the architecture's got blown away'. That is the problem! Too many people regard design as some kind of magic dust that you sprinkle on at the end, when all the really important things are decided. A bit of patterned masonry here... a few dormer windows and

pitched roofs there... some trees and bollards... and the ubiquitous wall-to-wall red brick paving. This is happening everywhere. Good design has a lot more substance than that – it is about the entire physical make-up of the public realm and its subsequent care and management. Urban design is not a magic dust that can be sprinkled on to make everything look okay: it is an integral part of the planning and management of an area.

What has happened in London during the 1980s epitomizes the problem. I at once acknowledge that there are many good, or potentially good, things happening in London, at places like King's Cross, Broadgate, Covent Garden, Charing Cross, the South Bank, and many more, where a few enlightened developers are working with imaginative architects, urban designers, artists and craftsmen to produce better, more popular development. My concern is this: when you consider the public environment of Greater London as a whole, these schemes, despite the size of some of them, are not enough to rescue London.

If you want to see what, left to its own devices, the private sector produces, one need look no fur-

ther than the Isle of Dogs in London's Docklands. The British Government's flagship of Enterprise Culture Development and the urban design challenge of the century adds up to little more than market-led, opportunistic chaos – an architectural circus – with a sprinkling of post-modern gimmicks, frenzied construction of the ghastly megalumps of Canary Wharf and a fairground train to get you there. It is a disappointment to residents and workers. There was a necessary intermediate step between balance sheets and building, that got missed in the rush. It is called 'urban design'.

Both political commitment and public investment are required. Ministers are rarely persuaded that there are votes in design or a good environment.

I cannot escape the conclusion that politicians have not got their priorities right in terms of our long-term needs. I also conclude that considerable public investment is urgently required to complement what the private sector is prepared to do.

And, where does the activity of town and country planning fit? Professor Colin Buchanan, in the *Report of the Commission on the Third London Airport*, wrote:

> Planning was born out of back-to-back houses, out of overcrowding, out of privies in back yards, out of children with nowhere to play, out of ribbon development and urban sprawl, out of countryside despoiled and monuments destroyed. It was born out of painfully gathered experience over a century of industrialisation which made it abundantly clear that market forces in land, left to their own devices, fail utterly to produce a humane environment.

What we now have to recognize, somewhat soberly perhaps, is that, operated in a highly legalistic and cumbersome, supposedly democratic context, planning has, for the most part, also failed to produce a humane environment. Why is this? What can be done to improve the situation?

It is not the planning system *per se* which is at fault. We need a strong planning system. It is possibly the way that it is operated that needs review. There needs to be greater sensitivity in the application of planning laws – better control over the location of high buildings, greater regard for historic areas, better understanding of the organic growth of towns and a striving for ever higher quality in

Left to its own devices, the private sector does not usually produce people-friendly environments, as the opportunistic chaos at the Isle of Dogs in London's regenerated Docklands demonstrates only too well.

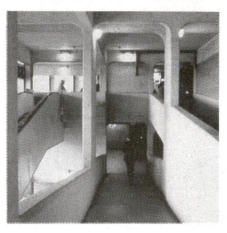

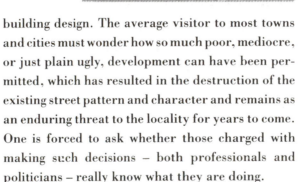

Why has so much indifferent, unfriendly and often plain ugly development been allowed in our towns and cities? Why is so much new development impermeable and hostile? Why have we been so keen to push pedestrians underground or up on decks? Why does that twentieth century urban phenomenon – the multi-storey car park – invariably produce such a depressing internal and external environment?

building design. The average visitor to most towns and cities must wonder how so much poor, mediocre, or just plain ugly, development can have been permitted, which has resulted in the destruction of the existing street pattern and character and remains as an enduring threat to the locality for years to come. One is forced to ask whether those charged with making such decisions – both professionals and politicians – really know what they are doing.

In New York and some other cities, the opening up of ground floors to public use is viewed as a public benefit, which often brings to the developer a bonus of additional floorspace and storeys. The planning system should not need to rely upon such crude horse-deals. The contribution that a development makes to the public realm is not some kind of negotiable afterthought – it is probably the most important factor about the development. Yet acceptance of that single statement will require a complete reorientation of development and planning attitudes throughout the world. Planning permission, quite simply, should never be granted unless the proposed development clearly enhances the public realm and provides, where appropriate, facilities and ameni-

ties for pedestrians at street level.

Planning should be more than short-term expediency in land sales and subsequent development. Boom–bust development cycles – three years of frenzied growth followed by five to ten years recession – are enormously damaging to the townscape of a city. Towns and cities need to be able to invest with confidence in a medium to long term future. While good opportunities should be seized as they arise, they should not be allowed to jeopardize worthwhile, longer-horizon commitments.

The planning process cannot be divorced from issues of architectural quality and maintenance of the built environment. The Report *How Do You Want to Live?* included the following statement, written in 1972:

> *'Mediocre, appalling, inhuman, banal and boring',*
> *are only a few of the adjectives used by our contributors to describe modern architecture as seen by people in towns and cities all over the country. The instant reaction is seldom wrong about architecture or people. The fact that people cannot explain precisely in architectural terms what is wrong does not necessarily make the building right.'*

It is actually awfully easy to recognize bad examples of urban development. In most instances the

authors of those schemes have not set out to create bad examples, which will be hated and reviled by the public. The fact is that it is very difficult to recognize and promote the ingredients of good development ahead of actual implementation. This book in part looks at why so many cities and towns around the world have become hostile to people and then, more importantly, considers in detail the ways in which this can be reversed – making our towns and cities once again *people-friendly*. Cathedrals and great palaces are rarely commissioned today. It is the *everyday buildings* in towns and cities that now matter most. They influence the character and quality of the place. It is by them that future generations will judge us.

Looking after towns and cities also includes *after-care* – caring about litter, fly-posting, where cars are parked, street cleansing, maintaining paved surfaces, street furniture, building facades and caring for trees and planting. After-care matters every bit as much as getting the design right in the first place.

Also, as we all become more sensitive to the delicate ecological balance of the planet, recycling of usable materials needs to be provided for in urban areas. Paper, card, glass and plastic can now be recycled. For example, in Italy, even very small rural towns and villages have recycling bins. How many other countries can make the same claim?

Much harm has been done, especially during the past twenty or thirty years. It is almost too late. But I believe the decline of the public realm can be halted and reversed if we – politicians, professionals and the community – are prepared to commit to a new set of objectives and a new agenda for caring about our urban areas – particularly the central areas of towns and cities, which of late have become so squalid. Above all, we must care again about the design, management and maintenance of the *public realm*.

Why does 'after-care' get so little attention, when all around us the public environment is polluted by litter, graffiti, fly-posting, vandalism and wilful neglect?

François Zbladin, Bruxelles 1989

2

'Places' Matter Most

When you get there, there isn't any there there.
Gertrude Stein on *Oakland, United States*

Places matter much more than either individual buildings or vehicular traffic. Yet, all over the world, our planning endeavours seem to concentrate almost exclusively on the latter considerations. We seem to be losing the ability to stand back and look at what we are producing as a whole. Most of us can think of collections of roads and buildings that simply do not add up to anything at all. We need to stop worrying quite so much about individual buildings and other individual physical artifacts and think instead about places in their entirety. We need to forget the spaced-out buildings of the past few decades, separated from each other by highways and left-over tracts of land. These unthinking, tired solutions to development have not served us well. We must concentrate on attractive, intricate places related to the scale of people walking, not driving. We must exploit individuality, uniqueness and the differences between places. An attractive public realm is very important to a feeling of well-being or comfort. Traditionally, building craftsmanship was not just about buildings, but also spaces. This should still be the case. Collaboration between all the environmental professions will be essential to achieve this.

The inescapable reality for all of us is that people judge the activities of architects and planners, landscape architects, highway engineers and civil engineers by the quality – principally the physical quality – of what they see and experience around them. And rightly so. Because, at the end of the day, it is the *product* rather than the *process* that matters most to the users. For all manner of reasons and quite understandably, the judgement that they make is rarely a complimentary or favourable one – largely due to the legacy of several decades of Modernist planning.

There are signs of a new approach to architecture and planning – a fundamental change in approach from the days of ruthless Modernism. British architect Terry Farrell succinctly describes how in the Modernist approach the primary object was a building or some other physical artifact. It was often separated from its neighbours by large tracts of land and/or highways – the left-over public realm. Designs were open and non-urban in character. The modernists obsessively and rigorously applied concepts of the grid, simplistic hierarchies, tidiness, low

The overriding criterion by which cities and towns should be judged is the nature of their public realm. The historic centres of Brussels, Belgium and York, England, are particularly 'people-friendly'.

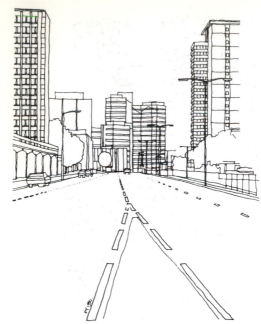

New environments are all too often characterized by spread-out mediocre buildings, lots of left-over space and rather uncomfortable arrangements for pedestrians. Such environments appear to be designed for the benefit of the moving vehicle and the property speculator and have devastated towns and cities all over the world, particularly when implemented on a so-called 'comprehensive' scale.

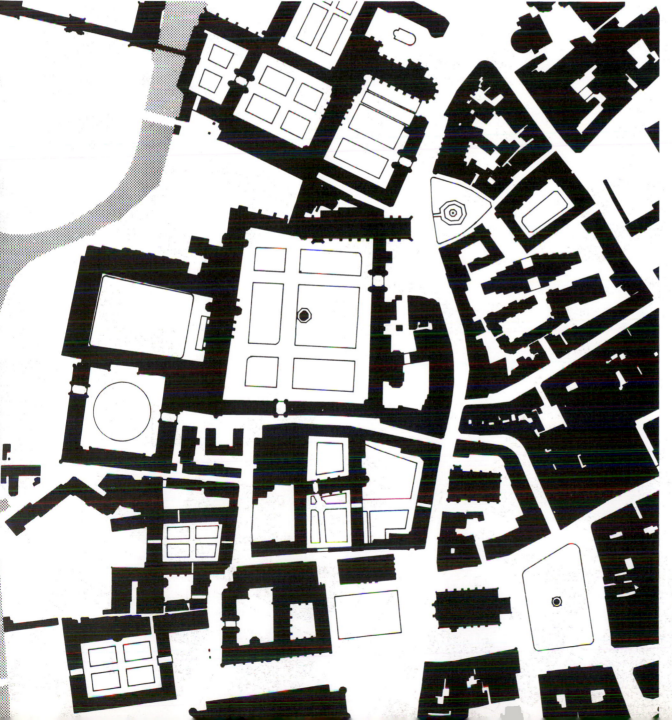

By contrast, traditional environments emphasize the spaces between buildings and usually produce an attractive, organic whole with a variety of useful pedestrian areas on a comfortable human scale. These two figure ground drawings relate to equivalent areas of urban land. The places they depict are only a two-hour drive apart – yet they could easily be on different planets!

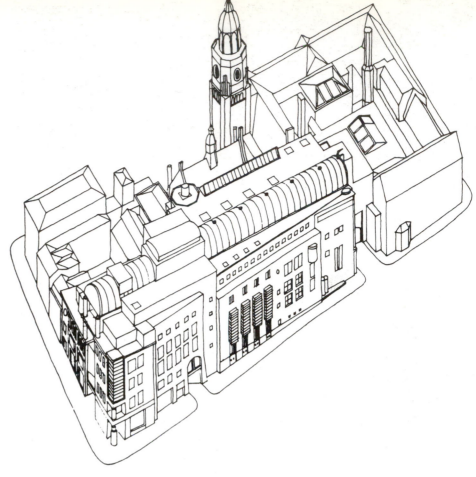

Proposals for new buildings, particularly infilling, should have a clear and positive relationship to the local architectural typology. This need not mean mindlessly copying it. Here are London examples of new West End streetscape and the remodelling of Croydon Town Hall for multiple public uses.

densities, zoned separation, the international style, large-scale engineering, a severance with history and tradition, high technology construction and mechanization. They thought at the scale of a moving vehicle. Growth and comprehensive redevelopment were the norm. Unconstrained, green field or war-damaged sites were the ideal canvas.

The devastation that this approach has produced on the public realm can now be seen in virtually every town and city in the United Kingdom and in many other countries too. A strong rejection of this philosophy is now emerging. We are witnessing a return to the spirit of urbanism that characterized well-loved traditional towns and cities. The concern is once again for the scale of people walking, for attractive, intricate places and for complexity of uses and activities. The object has now become the public realm -- the space between buildings – rather than the buildings themselves. The aim is to create urban areas with their own identities, rooted in a regional and/or historic context. The physical design of the public domain as an organic, colourful, human-scale, attractive environment is the over-riding task of the urban designer.

On urban sites, then – both in town and city centres and in inner city and suburban areas – we need a proper *urban* solution, with an *urban* scale. We need a clear appreciation of the urban grain and built form – what is sometimes called the morphological context. We also need to understand fully the local architectural *typology* – related to the uses and functions of the particular buildings. New proposals – whether for a large piece of urban design or an individual building – must have a positive relationship to the existing morphology – by harmonizing with it, by adapting to it or, where there are clear reasons so to do, by contrasting with it. The important thing is to take a positive design stance not just an arbitrary one.

During the 1950s and 1960s many towns and cities around the world underwent change on an unprecedented scale in terms of built development and in terms of massive highway construction. This undoubtedly resulted in considerable commercial vitality and unique levels of accessibility for motor vehicles, but it is now fairly widely recognized that it also produced physical environments that fall a long way short of current public aspirations.

Much of the problem derives from the loss of urban scale or grain. Traditionally cities were composed of blocks of buildings with streets around them. The so-called *comprehensive redevelopment* schemes of the past twenty or thirty years have tended to destroy this familiar and successful urban form and the results have been largely unsatisfactory. They have rarely produced places which are now widely recognized as being attractive.

It is a useful exercise to compare the plan forms of towns over time. Most traditional towns and cities are compact and tightly organized with a simple block layout punctuated by hard and soft open spaces. In many places this clear structure was lost, or significantly eroded, during the middle part of the twentieth century. A combination of war damage and the desire for new roads, new shopping centres and various forms of mass housing has, in many instances, led to the loss of original street patterns.

We don't have to let this happen. As vacant sites are brought into use and obsolescent buildings are redeveloped, the opportunity must be seized to use the new buildings to create proper urban streets again, with proper frontages – to make a tight-knit urban fabric where public spaces and landscape are intended, rather than just being the left-over bits that were of no use to the architect or developer. Spaces left over after planning and development has taken place are not only visually unattractive and functionally useless: they are also awkward and expensive to maintain, with the all too frequent result that they become neglected and unkempt. There are thus functional and environmental advantages to the restoration of the street.

Of course, it is not only streets that are important. The places that make up the public realm come in many shapes, sizes and uses. They include streets, squares, public footpaths, parks and open spaces and extend, also, to riversides and seafronts. These places all belong to the wider community. It is important never to forget that they are there for their use, benefit and enjoyment. In designing and developing buildings and environments which interrelate with the public realm, it is therefore essential to ensure that this tremendous value of the public realm to the wider community is acknowledged, respected and enhanced. This book makes some suggestions about ways of achieving this.

The 'public realm' includes streets and squares, alleyways and waterfronts – in short, all the places to which the public have physical and visual access.

One of the joys of towns and cities is their variety. Different areas have different characteristics – of activities, scale, uses and function. Some places are lively and busy. Others are quiet and secluded. There will be intricate, dense areas; open, monumental areas; soft areas; hard areas; old areas; new areas; areas of high building; areas of low building; shopping areas; commercial areas; entertainment areas; recreation areas; and so on and so on. We need to recognize this variety – to define areas of cohesive character. Often such areas will have blurred edges. They will overlap. This simply adds to the richness of the environmental character. But, great care is also required. As places, precincts or areas of special character are recognized, defined, created or developed, it is important to ensure that they are real and not contrived. It will not be an asset to the town or city if they take on a fake-believe or stage-set quality. Nor should such areas be allowed to develop simply as single-use enclaves.

All too often towns and cities simply continually re-adapt to accommodating more and more traffic and bigger and bigger buildings. What is desperately needed is a new approach to producing and looking after good urban spaces. We have actually got to address the re-structuring of our urban areas, over possibly quite long time scales, to reflect a new set of priorities in which the needs of people – as pedestrians, cyclists, the young, the old and the infirm, as well as the able-bodied – take precedence over the voracious demands of traffic and developers. The current fragmentation of urban areas in many ways mirrors the fragmentation and separation of the professions who are supposed to be looking after them – urban planners, traffic engineers, landscape architects, land surveyors and architects in particular. Greater multi-professional collaboration would, I am convinced, produce better, more coherent places, because no one profession has all the answers to the complex task of designing livable cities.

Public places within a town belong to the people of that town – they do not belong to developers or investors, the police or traffic wardens. Their nature will be influenced by their scale, shape and size; the ways in which they are related one to another; the uses and activities which they contain, and the way in which traffic of all kinds is handled.

Much of the pleasure of urban areas derives from the variety to be found therein – rich differences of style and character. Coming upon the Centre Pompidou in Paris from narrow traditional streets never fails to delight.

Francis Tibbalds, Centre Beaubourg, Paris

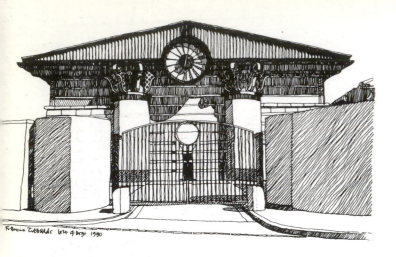

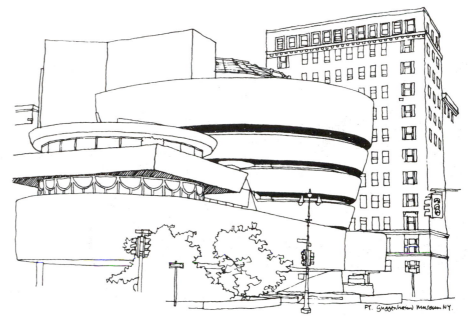

Ft. Guggenheim Museum NY.

There are occasional needs for the unusual, 'prima donna' set piece – like John Outrams's Pumping Station in East London or Frank Lloyd Wright's Guggenheim Museum in New York. The greater need is for a better vocabulary of well-designed, interesting 'backcloth buildings' like these examples from Berlin and London devised by architects Rob Krier, Richard MacCormac, Campbell Zogolovitch Wilkinson & Gough, and Jeremy Dixon.

The proper civilized use of places – streets, squares, alleys, promenades and so on – can be achieved visually, functionally and psychologically, through sensitive and imaginative design. If, for example, motorists feel like guests in a predominantly pedestrian area, hopefully they will behave like guests. Is this not infinitely to be preferred to a plethora of street signs and prohibitions backed up by tedious byelaws and penalties?

The same is true of buildings. New buildings are also guests in the existing urban environment and need to show due deference to their host and their companions. This is not to invite false modesty; nor is it to say that that there shouldn't be room for the occasional live wire or prima donna. What architects and clients need to accept, however, is that the greatest contribution that they can make to the built environment of the town or city is to construct good, backcloth buildings.

The challenge is clearly very great – finding ways of promoting the renaissance of the public realm in our towns and cities. But it is a potentially very rewarding and enjoyable one. It demands a new set of priorities in which, basically, *places* take prece-dence over buildings and traffic. This will be hard for the individual players to accept – be they architects, engineers or developers – if they maintain their professional separations. The more they learn to collaborate – to try to meet agreed, common objectives for the urban environment – the easier and more productive the process will become.

In the hope that it will be useful to readers, this and subsequent chapters conclude with short lists of recommendations, related to the theme of each chapter, which can be used at a checklist by practitioners.

Recommendations/action checklist

1 The first priority is to agree what sort of public realm is appropriate in any particular area and then to agree the buildings, development and circulation system which are appropriate to it. Usually this is done the other way round, with devastating results for the urban fabric.

2 Places need to offer variety to their users. They need to be unique and different from one another – each rooted in their own particular

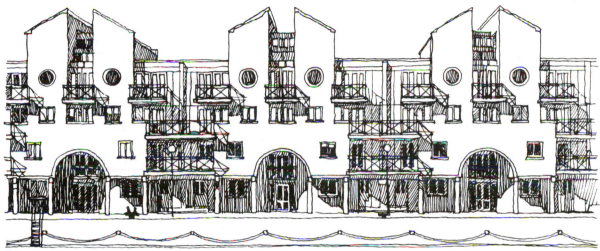

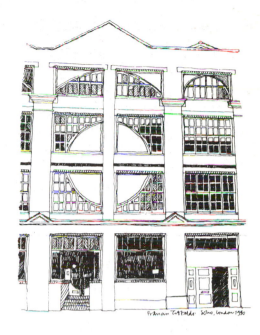

historical, geographical, physical or cultural context.

3   In most instances, individual buildings will be subservient to the needs and the character of the place as a whole. If every building screams for individual attention, the result is likely to be discordant chaos. A few buildings can, quite legitimately, be soloists, but the majority need simply to be sound, reliable members of the chorus.

4   Many town centres are small enough to be considered as single places. In the larger towns and the central areas of cities, over time, areas of different character are probably discernible. These should be defined and developed, providing they are for real, rather than artificial bits of make-believe or urban theatre that will, in the long run, devalue reality.

5   Try not to view the organization or reorganization of towns and cities purely from the rather exclusive points of view of the motorist or the developer. It is of greater importance to consider the needs and aspirations of people as a whole – with priority being given to pedestrians, children and old people. This simple change or widening of priorities could, by itself, transform our urban environment and lifestyle.

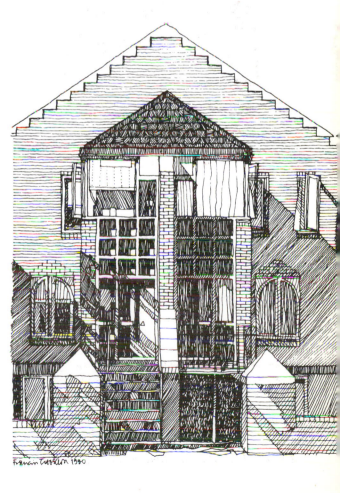

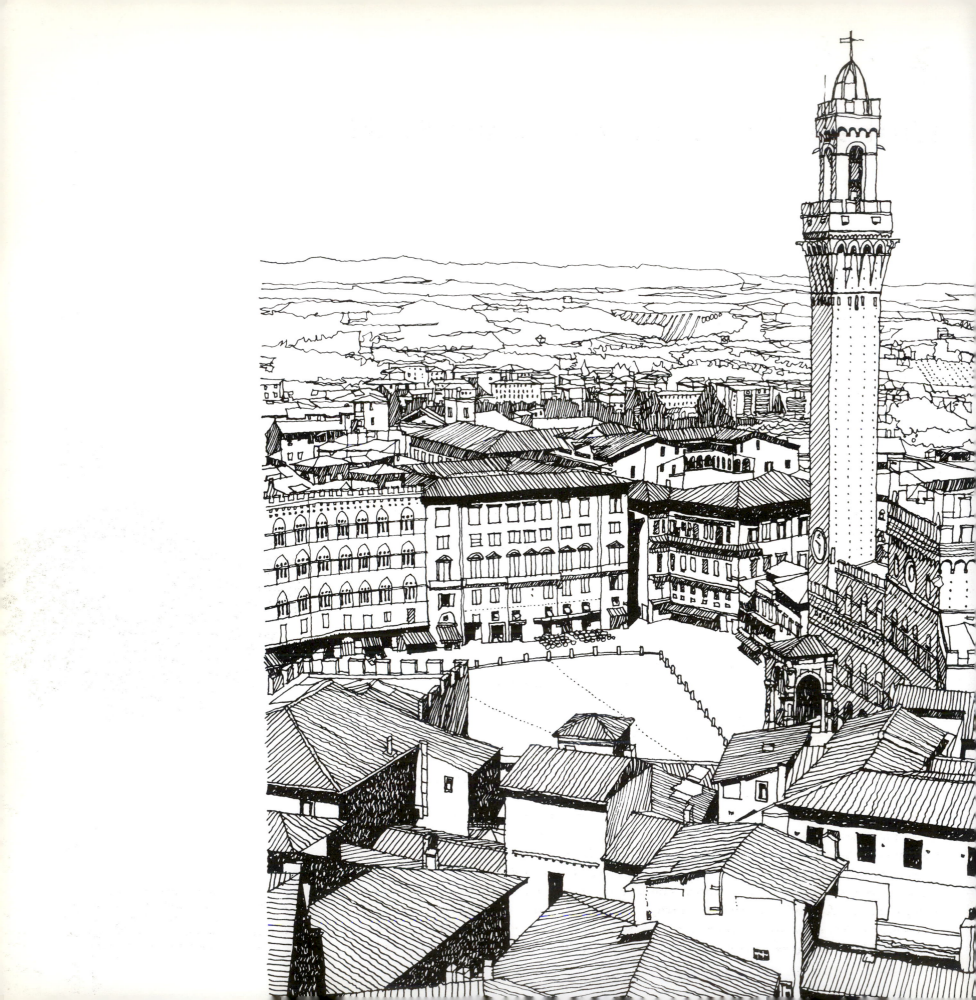

3

What are the Lessons from the Past?

*Those cities which have arisen more or less
spontaneously over many years are 'natural cities'.
Those cities and parts of cities which have been
deliberately created by designers and planners are
'artificial cities'. Siena, Liverpool, Kyoto, Manhattan,
are examples of natural cities. Levittown, Chandigarh,
and the British New Towns are examples of artificial cities.
It is more and more widely recognised today that there is
some essential ingredient missing from artificial cities.
When compared with ancient cities that have acquired the
patina of life, our modern attempts to create cities
artificially are, from a human point of view, entirely
unsuccessful.*

Christopher Alexander: *A City is Not a Tree.*

We can learn much from the existing context within which we work and from examples elsewhere. Traditional towns and buildings are generally put together far better than new ones. Why do they work? Why do people like them? Basically I think it is because they have certain essential qualities, like recognizable patterns and complexity within order. The question need to be posed, then, as to why new development should not have the same richness, individuality, intricacy and *user-friendly* qualities of existing places?

When we visit traditional well-loved towns – particularly in European countries – we tend to find them attractive, friendly and comfortable. Sometimes it is because they are smaller and therefore easier to take in and become familiar with. There are usually other characteristics in evidence too – the interesting exploitation of different levels; mixed uses; ordinary people actually living in the town centre, sometimes above their place of work or commerce; consistency or unity of materials – for example, the stone flags with which many Italian city streets are finished are a welcome relief from the acres of red brick paving that accompanies many

United Kingdom pedestrianization schemes; clear definition of the centre, for example, by walls; and of entrances thereto by gateways or arches which also functionally may restrict certain types of vehicular penetration; a distinctive skyline; a very permeable structure of alleyways and passages, often interestingly arched or vaulted over; small scale units – backcloth buildings of a consistent height against which special buildings are contrasted; large uses accommodated in modest buildings, as in the case of the narrow shopfronts in Florence, beyond which cavernous interiors exploit the depth of the block; views out, glimpses into courtyards, changing views, gardens and courtyards visible to the public; sharing of private space; and, the predominance of the public space.

Popular and attractive urban areas tend to be those in which a *contextualist* approach has prevailed. By that, I mean the process of examining the town or city as a whole and relating changes or new development to it in a sensitive and careful manner. This involves taking a comprehensive overview, but not in the sense of comprehensive redevelopment planning of the 1960s, much of which looks as though

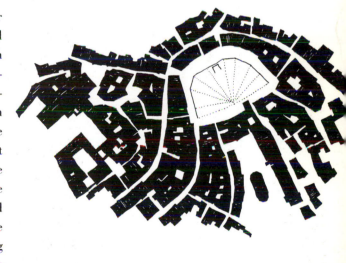

Siena – one of the most attractive, pedestrian-friendly cities in the world. There is no reason why new environments should not have the same rich, organic, individual qualities, without resorting to slavish reproduction of film-set townscape.

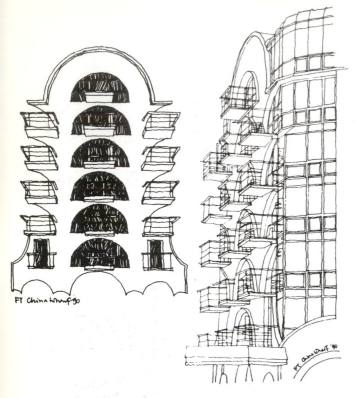

New buildings, like these from London's Docklands, must be obviously of their age. They should not have unimaginative graph paper facades.

We can learn much from places like Isfahan, Amsterdam and Nash's London all of which, by design or accident, exhibit a powerful organizing framework.

it has been carried out by a knife-happy, blindfold surgeon! Rather it is an urban healing objective, retaining as much as possible of what is good and worthwhile, and adding to it and enhancing it, with the aim of creating a new whole which is greater than the sum of its parts.

Over some 30 years of professional interest in town-making, I've come to accept, grudgingly at first, that traditional towns and buildings are usually put together far better than new ones. They have a richness, intricacy and user-friendly quality that has evolved from years, even centuries, of adaptation. That doesn't mean that I want new environments to be a pastiche of old ones, merely that I want us to examine how they work and why people like them and then to develop new urban forms and buildings which have those positive traditional qualities but are clearly of today.

New buildings must be imaginative and of high quality and, while being firmly rooted in or respecting their historical context, they must be obviously of their age. They must be decorative and interesting to look at: not bland, like the graph paper designs of the 1950s and 1960s, nor bits of classical pastiche

– a cop out which devalues history. The best architecture of all ages can usually live together, despite contrast of style, scale, use and materials. Above all, we must get well away from the bland International Style that has made so many capital cities all over the world begin to look so remarkably similar.

We need, then, a sound appreciation of the context of a project site or area. This includes its history, its existing townscape and appearance, its planning status and its social and economic role – both current and potential. The context should also include the client's objectives for the site or area.

All cities are different and reflect their time, place and the culture of their builders. Too many cities all over the world have spawned mediocre Western style development that have made their centres look remarkably similar. A few, designed centres have become just collections of fine individual buildings, often by eminent designers, which fail to come together to form a humane and meaningful whole. Brasilia, La Défence and New York's Lincoln Centre spring to mind as examples of the latter.

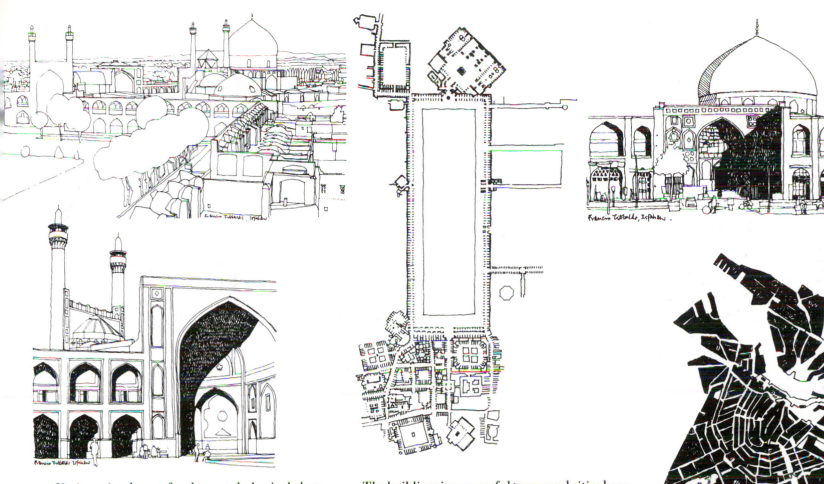

Various simple, yet fundamental physical characteristics are common to the centres of many of the world's best loved cities – London, Bath, Edinburgh, Paris, Amsterdam, Munich, Rome, Florence, Siena, Isfahan, Saint Petersburg, Peking, New York, Savannah, Chicago and so on. Such cities, whether their growth has been planned or developed organically, exhibit an *order for the whole*: blocks and streets, squares and courts come together to form a dense and interrelated pattern of buildings and circulation routes. This produces an urban design context made up of a limited number of standard units or solutions. Together, they form a larger whole in a variety of different ways, but which have a certain self-sufficiency in themselves.

There also exists in such cities a *greatness and variety of scale* and an *overlying hierarchy* in the arrangement of the main uses and communications networks, yet a flexibility to move these uses within the system. Between component sub-areas there is a combination of tight and loose fit, and the urban texture is dense enough to provide short walking distances so that pedestrians can move easily and in comfort from one place to another, close to buildings.

The buildings in successful towns and cities have a *consistency* in their design and materials, in which variety is achieved by a limited number of themes. As discussed in the previous chapter, quality in city design derives more from the nature and memorability of the spaces between buildings than from the buildings themselves. The street is the city's major public forum and its careful definition and design is a major element of urban design. This is examined further in Chapters 5 and 6. The special buildings on key streets are selectively designed and placed. Overall there should be an imaginative exploitation of the natural and topographical characteristics of the site and an emphasis on a generous and flexible circulation system that is not inextricably linked to any one mode. Finally, the designers of great and successful towns and cities – people like Sixtus V, Michelangelo, Sir Christopher Wren, Peter the Great, Baron Haussmann, John Wood, James Oglethorpe, John Nash – have all shown a particular approach which should characterize the design and implementation of urban proposals – a relentless dedication to putting design ideas to work for the benefit of the whole community.

Cities like Paris show us how prototypical building blocks can be used to produce consistency, unity and variety.

In addition to their considerable physical qualities, successful and attractive cities are also characterized by *a variety* and *mix of uses and activities* in any one area, as opposed to the modern principles of horizontal separation of use and activity. The next chapter explores the concept of mixed uses more fully. It is precisely the appeal of choice – of being able to live, work, recreate, shop and even find solitude in a single area – that has given many cities and towns their peculiar dynamic and their popularity. This mixing of the public and private, the special and the everyday, in a natural way, has led to cities and towns which people both love and enjoy using. Such a mix of uses – private commercial development as well as public institutional buildings, of daytime and night-time activities – must be a fundamental goal in designing and creating new people-friendly places.

New development should be part of a continuing tradition of town and city building. However, in a rich, historical context there is an obvious danger of superficial pastiche. New development should provide a contemporary response which is subtle, appropriate to the context and not self-conscious.

Acknowledging desirable historical precedents is not easy, in the context of accommodating the scale and nature of uses appropriate to a town or city centre in the late twentieth century and beyond. New buildings, for functional, economic and technical reasons, tend to be larger in bulk and height than traditional ones. Furthermore, they are less adaptable to change of use and the accommodation of multiple uses than their predecessors. Many famous cities – including Tokyo, Paris and London – are rapidly being emasculated by the proliferation of similar, high-rise buildings. The influences of economics, commercialism, modern technology and present-day modes of living and business, as well as those of architectural or popular fashion, take precedence over a more sensitive regard for the special nature of each city in which the buildings are erected and have created styles of building which tend to give modern cities a remarkable similarity the world over. We must avoid the automatic, standard international solution and the ignoring or destruction of unique traditional values and qualities by drawing on appropriate historical precedents. Newer uses are often more acceptable if they

New building, such as that depicted in Geneva, can be part of a continuing tradition of urban townscape, without resorting to pastiche.

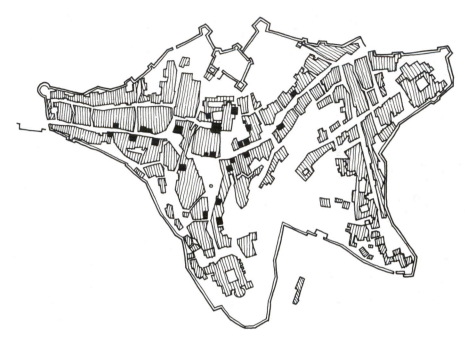

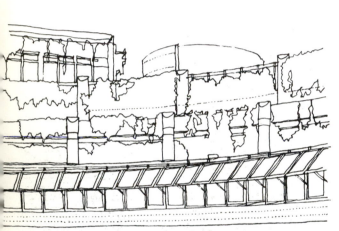

The diagonally-related public spaces of San Gimignano in Italy are a successful urban structuring device that can be traced through city planning over the centuries, right up to the recent development of London's Broadgate.

are constructed of traditional materials and we should not hesitate to find inventive ways of using stone, brick and tile whenever appropriate. But, at the same time, we must take full advantage of the possibilities offered by materials such as reinforced concrete, complex glass and glazing materials, steel and plastics, which the builders of older cities did not have at their disposal.

There are several design themes and concepts that have been historically well tried and proven. The most important, and tying all the rest together, is an underlying and perceptible sense of *order and unity*. We need to provide spaces and places that people remember. Stepped figure of eight spaces work well, as, for example in Versailles and the squares of San Gimignano, Venice and even Broadgate, London. Closely associated with this is the accentuation of *contrasts* – between soft and hard landscaping, between narrow streets and larger public spaces, between busy areas and quiet retreats, between colourful and patterned buildings and even monochrome ones, between town and country, between backcloth buildings and special or monumental buildings and so on. A centre primarily

composed of public and governmental buildings must also make room for more humble uses such as cafes, pavilions and kiosks and transient uses like exhibitions, tents and ceremonial decor.

Closely associated with the theme of contrasts is that of *variety and mix*. The historical precedents of Rome and Paris and the Georgian and Regency towns of England and Scotland suggest that environmental richness and variety derives more from diversity in the arrangement of buildings and land uses than it does from the buildings themselves, which should conform to simple principles of consistency in materials, details and facade design. Environmental diversity, then, can derive from the spaces between buildings – from the intricate ubiquity of the pedestrian network, the complexity of any slopes and changes in the ground level plane, from the adoption of an urbane mixture of scales and uses, from the development of the urban area as a series of linked, but different places, from the formal and informal hierarchies and referencing systems which relate one part of the city to another and from the interplay of near and distant views which open up to the citizen or visitor moving through the area.

The achievement of an early sense of *maturity* is a design theme which inevitably stretches the imagination, inventiveness and ingenuity of urban designers. Design at both the conceptual and detail levels must aim to shorten the period of newness and barrenness of appearance, so that the new development appears to have evolved naturally or organically. The provision of generous landscaping usually helps, as does careful phasing to avoid the image of the perpetual building site.

Wherever possible, designers should be dissuaded from inventing new and different solutions to essentially similar problems. Instead, *prototypical designs and details* should be adopted suitable to the particular context, using an appropriate common vocabulary – for example, of arcade forms, column and pier forms, ceiling and vault forms, building entrances, facade proportions and components. This is not quite the same as the so-called pattern book approach which is often advocated. Pattern books may have worked well traditionally for building town houses. I doubt very much that they could be devised in a manner that would work well for whole town and city centres.

Recommendations/action checklist

1 A clear and comprehensible framework and organization must be devised, to which the various public and private agencies involved in implementation can relate.

2 A series of simple design rules and principles should be developed.

3 There must be strong and passionate commitment to quality, completion and maintenance from the town or city's leaders: no great city has been realized without the support of strong individuals.

4 Designs and plans should avoid factors which militate against achievability – such as placements of land-uses and communication routes (the *traffic architecture* of the 1960s) in complex, single-purpose or inextricably close relationships to each other.

5 Old buildings will usually be devalued by copying, pastiche or facadism (the practice of retaining only the facade of an old building and developing a completely new structure behind it).

Variety and mix in style, height and bulk can produce great environmental richness as illustrated by examples from Siena and Amsterdam.

The presence of people on the street – from the simple Chinese shoemaker in Beijing to hoards of tourists in Amsterdam – make for lively, interesting, public environments.

and cities, security, contentment and even excitement come from the presence of lots of other people going about their business, enjoying their surroundings and presenting no threat. Think of much of Central Paris, Rome, Amsterdam, Chicago, San Francisco and many other bustling cities.

How can this busy quality be encouraged? My assertion is that it is directly related to the nature of the uses accommodated in the town or city and the degree to which they are mixed. Uses and activities are more important than buildings to the life of a town or city. Greater diversity will help to create a more livable city. Some European cities are now demanding, and achieving, 50–75 per cent residential floorspace in all central area developments. And, of course, the consequent higher densities bring other benefits – more efficient public transport and fewer private car trips, greater energy efficiency and better access and proximity to services and amenities like shopping, schools and social facilities.

The re-creation of a rich and diverse public environment is one of the urban designer's most important tasks in late twentieth century society.

It is my view that environments are necessarily complex, intricate and lively and are undermined by the over-simplification of land uses or activities and the dull uniformity of some built development. We must aim to produce environments which are of a mixed-use nature and are of a deliberately rich and varied character.

This seemingly obvious concept is not one that has found much favour with recent generations of city planners. The famous plans by such as Abercrombie, Le Corbusier, Lutyens and Howard, as well as those by the less famous, are characterized by an obsessive devotion to simplistic single-purpose zoning and segregation of uses. It was an essential part of the Modernist ethos. The results can now be seen most clearly in planned new communities and areas which have been totally reconstructed, for example, after war damage. The first of the British New Towns and reconstructed cities like Plymouth and Portsmouth in the United Kingdom and Pittsburg and Detroit in the United States are typical of this approach.

The Commission of the European Communities in its Green Paper on the Urban Environment recognizes

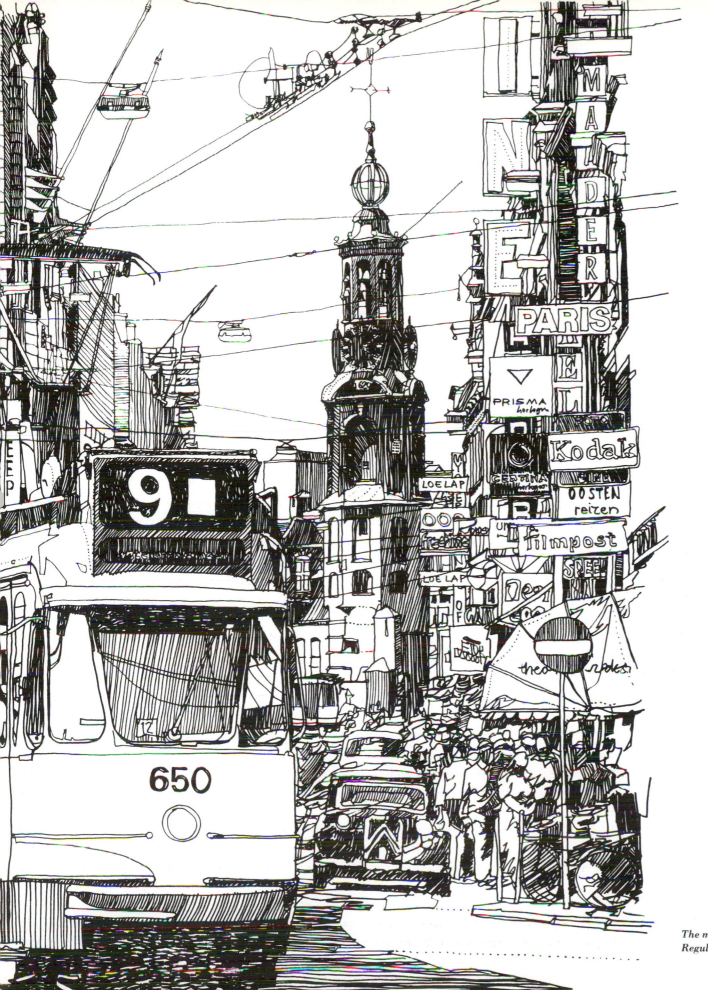

The mixing of uses should apply to whole streets, like Reguliersbreestraat in Amsterdam...

JUBILEE HALL
SPORTS CENTRE
JUBILEE MARKET HALL
JUBILEE HALL
SPORTS CENTRE
30 THE PIAZZA
COVENT GARDEN

...to single building complexes, like the Jubilee Hall in London's Covent Garden, which houses (in new and refurbished accommodation) a sports centre, a market, shops, restaurants and bars, offices, flats and roof gardens.

the evils of the strict zoning policies of the past twenty or thirty years – the separation of uses and the subsequent development of extensive peripheral residential suburbs have in turn stimulated commuter traffic, which is at the heart of so many of the difficulties now faced by urban areas. The Commission urges a review of zoning policy and the adoption of strategies which encourage mixed uses and denser development, so that people can easily live closer to their work places and, as in the Netherlands, the car can become an option rather than a necessity.

The concepts of zoning complexity and diversity are not ones which have been easily embraced by city builders – whether architects, planners or developers – in recent decades. But haven't we all always enjoyed the mixed use character of traditional urban areas, where the typical High Street building block consists of ground floor shops with offices and residential accommodation on the upper floors? Yet in many of those High Streets the floors over the shops are now substantially vacant – an appalling waste of existing resources, particularly when, in many cities, there are still so many people without the basic human requirement of a home of their own.

Jane Jacobs wrote cogently and convincingly in 1961 about the very essence of urban life and quality, out of alarm at what was happening to United States cities on reconstruction, in her marvellous book *The Death and Life of Great American Cities*:

> *Most city diversity is the creation of incredible numbers of different people and different private organizations, with vastly differing ideas and purposes, planning and contriving outside the formal framework of public action. The main responsibility of city planning and design should be to develop – insofar as public policy and action can do so – cities that are congenial places for this great range of unofficial plans, ideas and opportunities to flourish, along with the flourishing of the public enterprizes.*

As an impressionable architectural student, I found what she said immensely compelling and since then I have remained unshakeable in my belief that the best urban places offer a mixture of uses and a variety of activities and experiences. Zoned separation of uses literally kills urban areas. The most attractive places offer a variety of activities and experiences. Living, working, trading, shopping

City of London from Unilever House Francis Tibbalds April 1982.

and playing all gain from being linked. Mixed uses make for lively, safe environments – whether in whole streets or individual buildings. The public realm is safe and enjoyable because it attracts different people at different times for different purposes. This not only makes for lively environments, but it also provides informal surveillance of the public realm. Traffic can be part of it. Some streets have been totally emasculated by being pedestrianized in a crude and bland manner. The Dutch have done very much better in developing the *woonerf* concept in which essential traffic is not totally excluded, it is just tamed or calmed, by a variety of simple, but effective, physical measures.

It does not seem to me very difficult to get people to agree about the desirability of mixed use planning. I have heard the hardest-nosed developers extol its virtues and lament the fact that all the interesting and lively uses are being planned or zoned out of their favourite areas. The same developers will then bitterly defend their latest single-use development – usually for offices – with the plea that financial and funding institutions will not countenance mixed uses.

The fact of the matter is that if the will is there – by city planners and by developers – it can be done. In London's Covent Garden, the refurbished Jubilee Hall houses a gym and Sports Centre. The same building complex accommodates a market, shops, offices and flats. It even includes roof gardens, with planting visible from the public square below. I have never heard it suggested that, even in the context of Central London's very high land values, this development has not paid its way quite handsomely.

Are there simple rules for encouraging mixed uses? Scottish architect Charles Strang made to me the case for insisting on an element of housing in urban development, declaring that :

Much like the civilising impact of women in society, I have always thought that if one insisted on an element of housing in any development, the environmental impact of it would be softened.

He suggested that providing a percentage of any development site as housing would not be enough, since it would too easily end up as a monoculture with a blip of housing in one corner. He found rather

Examples from London's West End and the City of London itself show how, in the former, broadcasting, religion, tourism, medicine, residences and the professional institutions, and, in the latter, the law, journalism, education, commerce and religion, come together in complex and intricate ways to create a rich and memorable townscape.

Mixed uses can be accommodated in individual buildings and structures like the Unité d'Habitation in Marseilles, which houses a complete small community and its needs and the Ponte Vecchio in Florence which combines a pedestrian bridge with specialist shopping facilities.

more exciting the notion that any housing provided should be occupied before the rest of the building:

After all, if it is not suitable to live in, it can hardly be suitable to visit or to work in.

Jane Jacobs defined four conditions for generating exuberant diversity in a city's streets or districts, which are so relevant to the thesis of this book that they are worth quoting in full:

1   *The district, and indeed as many of its internal parts as possible, must serve more than one primary function; preferably more than two. These must ensure the presence of people who go outdoors on different schedules and are in the place for different purposes, but who are able to use many facilities in common.*
2   *Most blocks must be short; that is, streets and opportunities to turn corners must be frequent.*
3   *The district must mingle buildings that vary in age and condition, including a good proportion of old ones so that they vary in the economic yield that they must produce. This mingling must be fairly close-grained.*
4   *There must be a sufficiently dense concentra-*

tion of people, for whatever purposes they may be there. This includes dense concentration in the case of people who are there because of residence.

She had much to say about each of these conditions, but perhaps the most important was that each one was not enough by itself:

All four in combination are necessary to generate city diversity; the absence of any one of the four frustrates a district's potential.

I would extend that and say that they also need to exist in combination with the other generators of people-friendly towns described in this book.

In social and functional terms, most uses and activities can exist side by side or one above another. There will be exceptions – large-scale, noxious industry; uses attracting very large numbers of people and vehicles, such as a sports stadium; and, uses, like heavy manufacturing, which create noise, or a hospital that needs quiet environs for its inmates. But, on the whole, the majority of the uses and activities that make up a town or city – housing, employment, shopping, culture, entertainment,

Francis Tibbalds Florence 1990.

Macclesfield May 1988   Francis Tibbalds.

administration, public services and recreation – can exist cheek by jowl and the public urban environment will be the richer for it. Some cities already have the concept of mixed used zoning written into their development plans. The City of Westminster, for example, has a defined area of *central area uses* covering the West End of London. This needs to be promulgated elsewhere.

Longer shop trading hours, including at weekends, are a simple method to maintain life and vitality in a centre. Low rental buildings need to be deliberately provided in central areas to accommodate the specialized services and businesses that contribute so much to traditional urban areas but cannot afford the high rentals of new prime accommodation.

Traditionally, mixed use development of towns and cities has occurred in a largely organic and possibly accidental way. New ways need to be found to encourage this richness so that everyone benefits – individuals in the form of building owners; occupants and citizens in the form of users and passersby. It will need new attitudes by both city planners and developers as well as a willingness for these two

groups to abandon confrontational attitudes in favour of closer and more positive collaboration. Mixed use developments should be encouraged, with particular attention to seizing opportunities to incorporate residential accommodation. Living in the heart of towns and cities can add character, providing problems of affordability, appropriate tenure and social infrastructure can be overcome. Locating residential accommodation adjacent to commercial development, rather than on top may often be functionally more satisfactory for developers and tenants, but this will depend on the nature of the site and the other uses being accommodated.

Recommendations/action checklist

For city planners:

1   Mixed use zones should be clearly defined in development plans, particularly related to central areas and nodes of activity.

2   Development briefs for specific sites should specify two or more uses, with particular reference to their contribution to the street level environment.

In many traditional towns, like Macclesfield, in the north west of England, mixed uses develop naturally or organically in a largely accidental manner.

3   The commercial development content for each site should be expressed as a range, with upper and lower floorspace limits. Provision of additional uses in a development – particularly housing, entertainment, cultural or social uses – should be a key criterion against which the upper quantum may be accepted – *the carrot*.

4   There should be a presumption against granting approval to single-use development or development of a predominantly single use – *the stick*.

For developers and funding institutions:

1   Developers and financial institutions need to adopt a more imaginative approach to the formulation and funding of projects whereby mixed use schemes are at least as attractive as single use schemes and can be easily sold on.

2   Regard should be had to the existing uses on sites being considered for assembly on the basis that such uses may not be automatically extinguished without adequate safeguards for their reinstatement, unless they are clearly obsolescent. New proposals must provide for more rather than less diversity of activity and public interaction.

3   Development proposals must demonstrate how different uses may be functionally satisfactorily accommodated on a particular site – vertically and/or horizontally. Uses must not be proposed at street level which have a deadening or sterilizing effect on the pedestrian environment, such as offices or blank walls to supermarkets or car parks.

4   Where the appropriate street level use cannot be achieved from the outset, the development should, nevertheless, be designed for its ultimate incorporation.

Francis TWKindt Cambridge 1989

5

Human Scale

Urban areas exist for human beings. They do not exist for cars or lorries or big constructional projects. This would not, however, be immediately apparent when wandering around the majority of our towns and cities. We need to find ways to give our urban areas this human quality or scale.

Fundamentally, a comfortable human scale environment is one which is related to the scale and pace of pedestrians, not to that of fast-moving vehicles. This does not mean that we should be thinking in Toy Town dimensions. Human scale need not necessarily be prejudiced by high buildings, provided these are carefully located, designed with a top and a bottom and have regard to the effects on the microclimate. Tower blocks are, however, an expensive, often uneconomic form of construction and should be discouraged where lower, deeper-plan form buildings are practicable. What is equally important is that the skyline of the town or city should not appear arbitrary or accidental – with buildings of different heights and shapes scattered randomly all over the urban area. It needs to be properly designed. Town planners and urban designers are quite familiar with addressing the town or city on

plan – all they need to do is the same thing in section or elevation.

Buildings are, of course, perceived at different distances. But, getting it right close to eye level – close to people walking about – is particularly important. It is largely at this level that we achieve, or fail to achieve, human scale in a place. Building heights are not unimportant, but they are relatively easy to deal with. Height limitations can be set for particular contexts, with exceptions for buildings which, by virtue of their use or form, make a positive contribution to the skyline as landmarks. But it isn't just height that matters in consideration of human scale. In parts of Manhattan, for example, a pleasant pedestrian environment has been achieved by the way in which the street level is handled – it being largely irrelevant whether the main building rises to ten, twenty or a hundred storeys. Equally a four or five storey building can be totally alienating to the pedestrian environment if it fits unhappily with its neighbours or provides a dull, ugly or unfriendly street level facade. Go and walk round the bottom of the new Lloyds Building in the City of London. Whatever the building's other merits, by no stretch

Getting it right close to eye level is all important – whether in the intricate streets of Cambridge, England or an unusual drug store in Montreal, Canada.

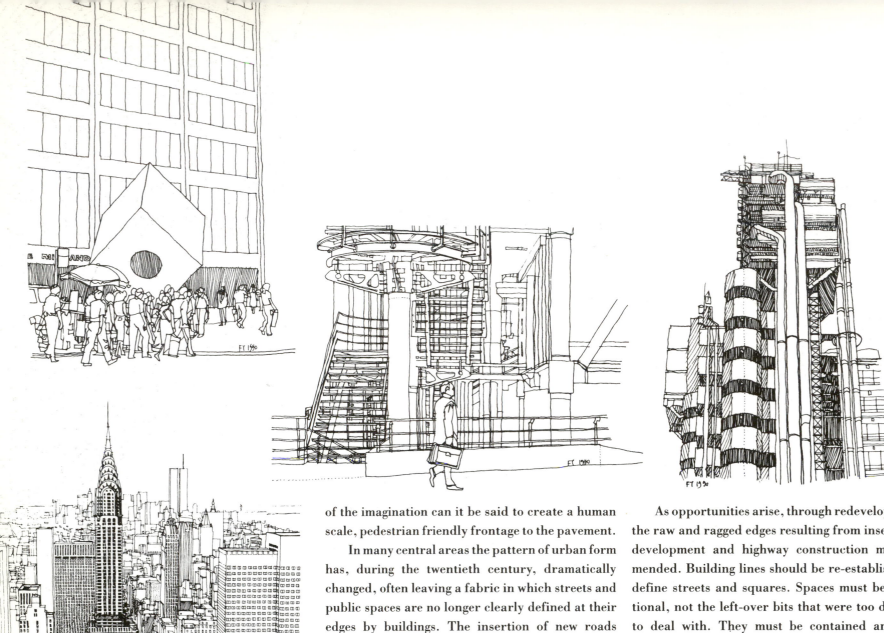

High buildings need not be incompatible with achieving a pleasant street-level environment as we learn from New York's Manhattan, but, whatever its other attributes as a bit of shiny sculpture on the skyline of the City of London, many would agree that the new Lloyd's Building gives nothing very much to the adjacent pedestrian environment.

of the imagination can it be said to create a human scale, pedestrian friendly frontage to the pavement.

In many central areas the pattern of urban form has, during the twentieth century, dramatically changed, often leaving a fabric in which streets and public spaces are no longer clearly defined at their edges by buildings. The insertion of new roads invariably leaves wounds or gashes through the urban fabric, with a surfeit of uncared-for, left-over space, vacant sites, temporary car parks and buildings facing the wrong way or set back too far from the road. Such places are ugly and unpleasant – they have lost the human scale which is vital to successful urban areas.

We need to re-establish the importance of the street as a key component in the urban fabric. All too often the streets and street pattern of a town or city have been destroyed by internal shopping centres and comprehensive development schemes. Their impact on the townscape has invariably been a damaging one. They have tended to produce lots of blank or bland frontages, facades set back from the street edge and many awkward, ill-cared-for, left-over spaces.

As opportunities arise, through redevelopment, the raw and ragged edges resulting from insensitive development and highway construction must be mended. Building lines should be re-established to define streets and squares. Spaces must be intentional, not the left-over bits that were too difficult to deal with. They must be contained and well defined. Public and private areas, and fronts and backs of buildings, must be easily recognizable. This is a familiar pattern, which people like and with which they feel comfortable. By comparison, the formless development of the 1960s has left a legacy of anonymous spaces which people find uncomfortable, ambiguous and disorienting.

As outlined in the previous chapter, a town or city centre draws its vitality from the activities and uses in the buildings lining its streets. In this respect the facades and activities provided at street-level – closest to eye-level – are particularly important. Too often new buildings have bleak and unfriendly frontages at street level. These deaden the adjacent area. The design customarily fails to provide for the potential later opening-up of a suitably active use at street level and consequently the facade remains

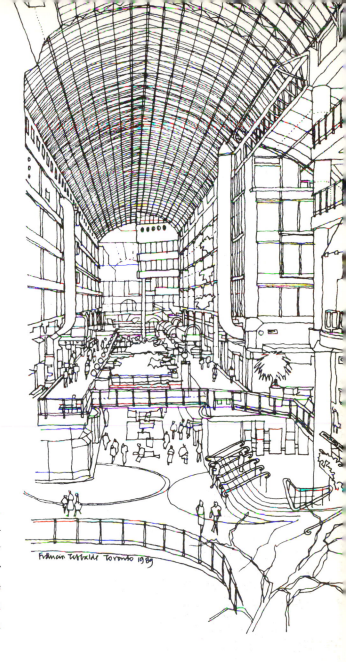

blank and unfriendly. As a minimum the design should indicate the function of the adjacent building – what goes on inside – and where to find the entrance should you need it. These are very simple requirements, indeed. Yet, it is quite remarkable how few buildings meet them.

Shopping is obviously a key pedestrian-level use. It can be combined with arcades, courtways and lanes to provide an attractive, semi-protected, human scale, pedestrian environment. It is one of the key activities and building blocks of central areas and should be exploited to the full for public benefit and enjoyment. What is, in my view, quite unacceptable, is the current, unthinking emulation of United States practice, in which whole city blocks are privatized to form internalized shopping malls, which are patrolled by security guards and close at 5.30pm and at week-ends.

The form of new buildings can also be a problem in the pursuit of the goal of an appropriate human scale. New buildings tend to be large and slab-like. They block pedestrian movement. We've got to find ways of making new urban environments permeable – encouraging a fine grain of pedestrian

movement through and between buildings. Arcades, passages and courtyards all help enormously. It also needs a more flexible attitude by building owners to providing public access on to or across their land. The next chapter deals with the need for freedom of pedestrian movement in urban areas, which is obviously closely associated with issues of human scale.

Many towns start off at an advantage. It is essential that they retain their traditional networks of small alleyways, little streets and lanes and the small-scale uses that are associated with these. They can be lost very easily on redevelopment, as bigger and bigger sites are assembled. We must guard against this. Opportunities need to be taken not only to retain and enhance what already exists, but also to extend it and to increase the permeability of the urban area.

The enclosure of urban space to make outdoor rooms is important not only to the achievement of human scale, but also to a general sense of protection and well-being. The range is enormous – from the grand square or piazza, formal collegiate quadrangles, the covered-in shopping street (like the Eaton

Shopping is a key pedestrian-level activity and usually combines happily with arcades to form semi-protected human-scale environments. Few modern shopping centres are legible and distinctive internally and have other than blank or bland outsides. The Eaton Centre, Toronto, is a welcome exception.

Francesco Tibaldi, Rome

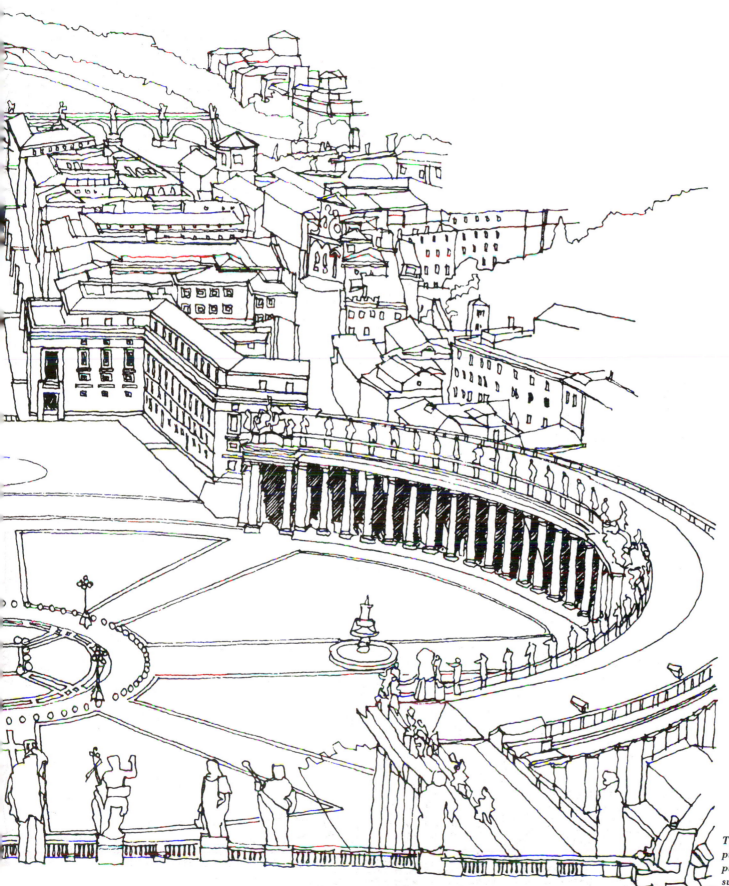

The enclosure of urban space to make outdoor rooms provides a human-scale environment and a sense of protection and well-being. The range extends from such grand spaces as St Peter's Piazza in Rome...

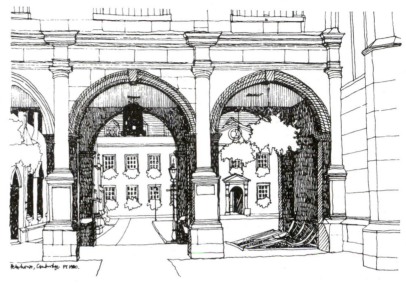

...to London squares, Cambridge quadrangles and New Mexican courtyards

Centre, Toronto) ... to small domestic courtyards (like those in Spain or New Mexico) and patios. Some will be wholly public: others semi-private, with public access limited by time or purpose of visit. Some will be wholly private, but capable of being glimpsed from the public realm and therefore capable of contributing thereto.

Human scale may be difficult to maintain where large or wide streets or spaces are pedestrianized. Many main streets take two, three or even four lanes of vehicular traffic. Exclusion of the traffic leaves a wide, empty space. It is essential not to be daunted or panicked by this. All too frequently the engineer or urban designer takes fright at the scale of the resultant space, after traffic has been excluded. There is a tendency to try and fill it up again as quickly as possible – not only with wall-to-wall red brick paving, but also all manner of street furniture, bollards, planters, seats, kiosks and spindly trees. The result can often look as though a giant had tipped out a box full of assorted exhibition products with the sole purpose of creating a visually chaotic, obstacle course for pedestrians. This is not the way to produce attractive public space. It does not pro-

vide a satisfactory human scale. The obstructions are also potential hazards – particularly to the old, disabled persons and blind or partially sighted people.

Although each situation should be examined and designed on its merits, the general advice should be to *keep it simple*. Stone paving slabs provide a surface which is more functionally and visually robust than the ubiquitous brick pavior. The latter is far more appropriate in smaller-scale locations and semi-private places like gardens and courtyards. Cobbles and granite setts have traditionally provided the same robustness and can readily be used, if appropriate, to provide an overall floorscape framework or design – by which I do not mean fussy, bit and piece patterning. The character and quality of the pedestrianized public space should derive, not from a Mickey Mouse collection of street furniture, but from the overall form and enclosure of the street, the views out of it and the nature of the uses and activities lining it. With respect to the latter, most uses can lend something to the public realm – attractive window displays, arrangements of produce or products on the pavement, provision for outdoor

Franim Tibbalds, Rome

The integration of pieces of art, as in Rome's Piazza
Navona, has for centuries enriched public space.

Public sculpture, in stone, metal, wood and clay can be found in many cultures, as these examples from Persia, China, Nigeria and Europe demonstrate.

eating and drinking, views in to what is happening inside the building, works of public art and simple, colourful displays of potted plants, shrubs and creepers. In streets of very generous dimensions, it may be appropriate to introduce groves or boulevards of suitable street trees or form a focus at the confluence of routes, possibly marked by a piece of civic sculpture or some other robust object. The key must be to maintain the *scale and integrity of the street as a whole*.

The integration of pieces of art on and around buildings has for centuries enriched public environments. This means that we should not only support such initiatives as the Percent for Art movement, but also recognize in our work a greater need for craftsmanship in building – to produce some of the rich and enduring qualities of traditional construction. It also means that in appropriate projects – which are likely to be large, mixed use and/or civic projects – we should endeavour to include relevant works of public art in, on, around or between buildings. This does not mean dumping a mediocre piece of stereotype sculpture in a square or entrance foyer as a token or afterthought. It means considering art

and decoration – whether sculpture, murals, carving, pattern, mosaic, architectural graphics or many other forms – as part of the design of the building or space. This means that the artist must become part of the design team – ideally as soon after the inception of the project as practicable.

Recommendations/action checklist

1 Developers of new buildings on important pedestrian routes and in public places, should seek to create an active and attractive pedestrian street frontage or, as a minimum, make provision for its future easy conversion.

2 Existing owners should be encouraged by the planning authority to create street level activity in existing dead frontages, especially on key pedestrian routes.

3 Buildings must not block pedestrian movement or key views.

4 High buildings must be located with care and have proper tops and bottoms. An impact study (for visual intrusion and effect on the microclimate) should be conducted for all high buildings (that is, those which are higher than

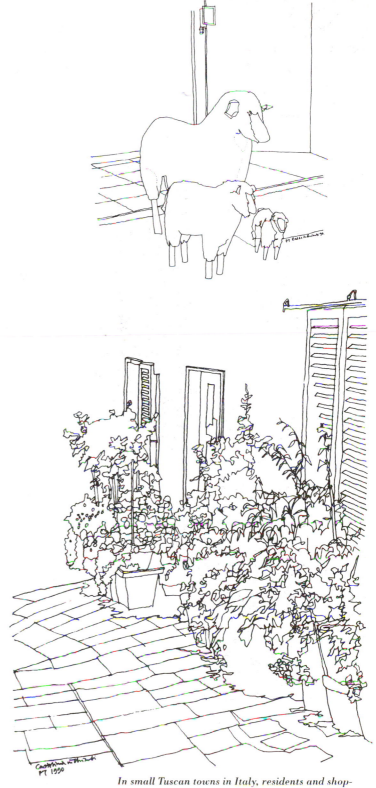

the average overall height of the surrounding area).

5   Traditional streets and street frontages should be preserved or re-established wherever practicable.

6   The design of pedestrianized public space will generally be more successful if it is kept simple and uncluttered. The key is to maintain the scale and integrity of the street or space as a whole.

7   At the inception of the project, consider whether there will be the opportunity for the incorporation of a work or works of public art.

In small Tuscan towns in Italy, residents and shopkeepers alike freely contribute to a more colourful and interesting pedestrian environment – for example, with abundant potted plants and hanging creepers and the eye-catching group of wooden sheep marking the entrance to a wine store in Radda in Chianti.

Francis Tibbalds San Gimignano 1980.

6

Pedestrian Freedom

*Pedestrians, on the whole, are not merely interested in
walking. They want to get somewhere and do something, and
they will not take kindly to planners who simply push them up
to the first floor to do their walking out of harm's way –
particularly when it entails ruining the appearance of many
streets and buildings, spending a great deal of money and
making them go a long way round as well. For this reason the
chief hope must lie in trespassing on street space at present
reserved for traffic, and converting it to pedestrian use.*

How Do You Want to Live? 1972

Few would disagree with the assertion, over 25 years
ago, by Sir Colin Buchanan (*Traffic in Towns* 1963)
that

> *...the freedom with which a person can walk about and
> look around is a very useful guide to the civilised quality
> of an urban area.*

But nearly three decades on, there are still many
obstacles to pedestrian freedom – basically deriving
from the way traffic is managed and the manner in
which buildings are formed and located.

Both pedestrians and cyclists face daunting hazards in most city and town centres. Apart from the
risk of accidents, noise and fumes are immediately
unpleasant and may cause longer term health problems. Traffic signals rarely discriminate in favour of
those on foot, who often have a mere few seconds to
cross in front of vehicles revving their engines in
anticipation of a quick get-away when the lights
change. Even in space exclusively reserved for
pedestrians, obstacles to safe, comfortable walking
come in many forms – posts, poles, bollards, seats,
litter-bins, advertising features, cars parked in
whole or part on the pavement, planting features

and tubs, broken paving, puddles, litter, debris and
sometimes even large holes.

We are still struggling to solve the problems
posed by motor vehicles, especially cars. We all use
cars. They are a very convenient mode of personal
transport. But they are killing our towns and cities.
As I've travelled around, I've been dismayed by the
extent to which cherished environments are being
eroded by cars and the clutter that goes with them.
There are cars everywhere. The old hill-top town of
Le Mans is very beautiful. Not content with filling
the old cobbled streets with parked cars, the French
have actually driven a road in a canyon right
through the heart of the historic city! Have we got
our priorities right?

As noted in the previous chapter, new buildings
tend to be large and slab-like. They block pedestrian
movement. Successful street level urban environments are *permeable* to pedestrians, that is they permit or encourage pedestrians to move about in a
variety of directions. Building forms which are
based on arcades, passages and courtyards draw
people through and between them and are interesting to walk by and look at close to eye-level. Some

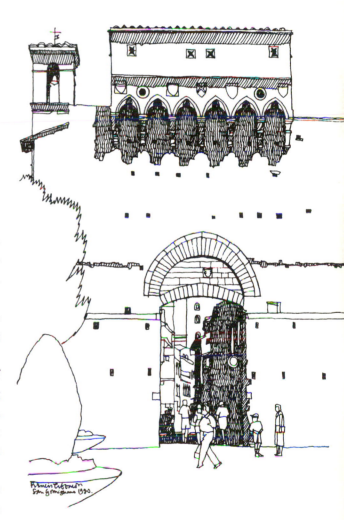

*The most pedestrian-friendly places offer a sequence
of experiences to the pedestrian or visitor – as in San
Gimignano, Italy, where the curving main street is
approached, through a comparatively small opening
in the town wall, denying a view of the town's squares
until the last minute.*

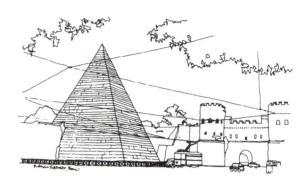

Unusual buildings or parts of buildings act as useful markers to help pedestrians find their way about a city – corner turrets from Le Mans, France and The Hague, the Netherlands, and the 12th century BC Caius Cestius Pyramid at the Porta S. Paola – marking one of the traditional entrances into the city of Rome.

degree of shelter from bad weather is generally welcome, together with convenient, safe opportunities to cross busy roads. However, on the whole, people have found totally enclosed pedestrian environments and underpasses or bridges rather uncomfortable, disorienting and alienating, preferring usually to remain at ground level and in spaces open to the sun, rain and sky. It is very important to keep people and activities at street level. Bridges, decks and subways are universally unpopular and are now being demolished in many cities. Moving around a city is easier where a limited number of routes act as main spines. These can be reinforced by the placing of landmarks or marker buildings; by facilitating physical and visual linkages; by encouraging appropriate street level activities in the adjoining buildings; by seeking design continuity through paving materials, street furniture and public art; by special or enhanced street lighting or floodlighting of buildings; and by the establishment of green or landscaped linkages along the routes. Tall buildings and corner buildings with memorable features are particularly useful to assist or guide pedestrians through a city.

Some central areas are easy to comprehend and to move around in, whether as a driver or as a pedestrian. Others, because of their physical extent, their traffic management systems or the barriers introduced by much insensitive highway engineering, are almost impossible, especially for the visitor. The more difficult centres cannot be sorted out overnight. However, over time, it is possible for the design and planning of urban areas significantly to contribute to making it easier to move around.

And what about cars? Well, quite simply, the attitude that we take to ever-increasing numbers of cars entering and passing through towns and cities is pretty central to the issue of pedestrian freedom.

What are the options? Well, we can *build more roads!* Road building is *not* the answer – it is colossally expensive, environmentally damaging and poor value for money. Most towns and cities already have far too many roads, choked with traffic. The lesson must be learned that traffic inexorably expands to fill all the space available, and as congestion is temporarily eased in one place, somewhere else becomes even worse.

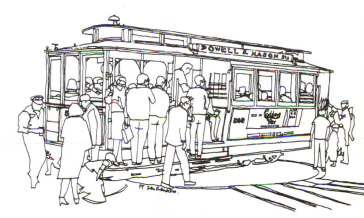

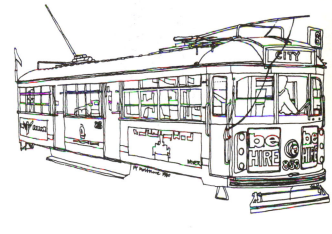

We can *move facilities* that generate lots of cars to out-of-town locations, close to good primary roads. Such developments tend to be very popular with shoppers, but display a devastatingly ugly environment externally. And what impact will out-of-town development have on the commercial viability of existing town centres?

Or we can apply policies of *constraint*. People can no longer expect to take their cars right into the heart of towns and cities. Basically this is the option that many local authorities are adopting. It can be achieved by *persuasion* – offering good public transport alternatives, including new modes of transport filling the gap between walking and using a bus or tram. Many countries invest heavily in public transport because it is good for the economy as a whole – one has only to look at the French Metro, the new RER and France's growing network of high-speed trains. At the same time Mayor Chirac is cancelling some 100,000 parking spaces in Paris as part of a plan to hand over much of the city to public transport and pedestrians. They are streets ahead!

Or we can decide to *penalize* the driver finan-

eially – high car parking charges, parking meters ... possibly, one day, road pricing.

We can do it by *compulsion* – altering the physical structure of the town, through pedestrianization and traffic management schemes (including road narrowing and roundabout-reducing) to make it impossible for cars to penetrate where we don't want them.... returning at least the city centres to pedestrians. There are now such schemes in most towns and cities. They are not without problems – they can be rather bland and empty, service traffic needs to be accommodated, car parks need to be woven into the urban fabric, the excluded traffic has to go somewhere – often it is squeezed into inner residential areas which weren't designed for it.

I don't actually think that there is a single solution. Some combination will be required to suit the particular circumstances. The first priority would seem to be to remove extraneous traffic – especially heavy lorries – from inner urban areas, and then to consider how best to deal with the proliferation of private cars. Governments must abandon short-term, *ad hoc* approaches. We need master plans laying down a timetable for co-ordinated, coherent

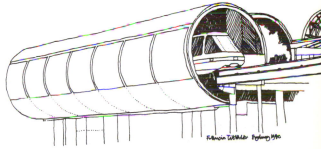

Sensible cities invest in and maintain good systems of public transport, such as the trams of San Francisco and Melbourne and the new monorail of Sydney.

The humble bicycle is becoming increasingly recognized as one of the most environmentally-friendly means of transport – found in particularly great abundance all over China, throughout the Netherlands and in the collegiate centres of Oxford and Cambridge, England.

investment to give towns and cities the public transport systems they require and the traffic calming measures now being successfully tried in many countries. Without such an approach, and some judicious discouragement of the private motorist, many towns and cities are simply going to choke to death.

Many towns and cities could easily be much more pedestrian-friendly than they are at present. Pedestrian streets should be extended; through traffic excluded and traffic calming techniques used to reduce the hazards and intrusion of motorized vehicles. Waiting times on pedestrian green phases at road intersections should be kept to a minimum. The complete exclusion of traffic, however, is not always a good thing – some traffic can give life and vitality to a city. It may, in some cases, be preferable simply to widen pavements. Sometimes, too, streets can be successfully shared between pedestrians and vehicles. Perhaps the best advice I can give to traffic engineers and planners is to make a study tour to the Netherlands and take a look at the *woonerf* concept. *Woonerven* are shared surface areas in which essential traffic movement is allowed, but, through the design of the street, it is subservient to the needs of pedestrians.

Above all, solutions need to be worked out jointly – not only through collaboration between the different professionals concerned, but also by collaboration between those professionals and the community. Engineers cannot be left to do it by themselves. As I've looked around at what highway engineers have done, I've seen a poverty of imagination – no trees, soul-less inhuman swathes of highway, no fun, no joy, no excitement. The first question to be asked must be – what sort of cities do we want?. We can then decide the appropriate transport system. It should not be done the other way round!

The concerns of the community are many – congestion, safety, passenger comfort, convenience, access for the disabled, pollution, visual intrusion, noise, congestion, vibration and so on. Those concerns have got to be communicated to Governments. Ministers will only listen if they think they are going to lose votes. It can be done. People must show their concern. It may be that damage to health is one of the best handles to hang it on. We must also think twice about second cars, driving cars with only one occupant or even having a car at all. We've all got to become more socially conscious and less selfish.

Salisbury, England – total exclusion of traffic may not be necessary for the creation of a pedestrian-friendly environment.

The arcade, in timber, brick, stone and steel, is a useful pedestrian-friendly device to humanize urban areas – examples from Melbourne Australia, Santa Fe in New Mexico and Soho and Covent Garden in London.

Jonathon Porritt has made a cogent argument for a *sustainability levy* – if you insist on having the personal freedom afforded by the private car, then you must be prepared to pay the full environmental costs in terms of congestion; accidents and fatalities; noise, dirt and deteriorating quality of life; environmental impacts, including the contribution to acid rain and global warming; and, respiratory illnesses caused by noxious fumes.

I started this chapter with Buchanan. Let me finish with him. Here is the last paragraph from the Report. It is entitled *The Creative Opportunity*:

Our studies indicate that the main creative opportunities for dealing with motor traffic will come in conjunction with the enormous task of urban reconstruction and expansion which faces this country.

This was, we must remember, over twenty-five years ago.

The pressures that are now developing – the increase of the population, the reaction against overcrowding and obsolescence , the increase of motor vehicles, the demands for industrial productivity, the continued drift of population and employment to the south, the rapidly increasing demands for holiday facilities – these are such

that, unless the greatest care is exercized, it will be easily within our ability to ruin this island by the end of the century. The greater part of it could easily degenerate into a wilderness of sprawled-out, uncoordinated development. On the other hand, given public understanding of the matters at stake, the smallness of the country could be an asset. Recreating the urban environment in a vigorous and lively way could do more than anything to make it the most exciting country in the world, with incalculable results for our welfare and prosperity.

Recommendations/action checklist
To everyone:

1   Think twice before taking a car into a central urban area.

2   Exert your right as a pedestrian to walk around freely.

To planners and engineers (and their political masters):

1   Politicians, traffic engineers and planners must stop giving permanent priority to the motor car and thereby assisting the destruction of the environment. They need to think like pedestrians, cyclists, the old, children and disabled persons, not just like drivers.

2   Keep people, as pedestrians, and related

activities at street level, as far as practicable.

3   Don't obstruct pedestrians with impenetrable buildings, walls, fences and other barriers to natural desire-lines.

4   Avoid over-reliance on single routes. A fine network of movement is needed, giving choice, variety and deliberate redundancy.

5   Reduce vehicular traffic to that which is appropriate to the use and the environmental quality of each street. This may sometimes lead to complete pedestrianization. Often, however, widened pavements, traffic-calming measures or shared vehicular/pedestrian space will be enough.

Francis Tibbalds Rome.

7
Access for All

You can dream, create, design and build the most wonderful place in the world ... but it requires people to make the dream a reality.

Walt Disney

When development takes place in our towns and cities it should seek to promote and accommodate the general health and well-being of its users in the widest possible sense.

It is important to ensure that we provide variety and choice in access to different activities, resources, information and places for all sectors of the community. Urban areas need to be accessible to all, regardless of age, ability, background or income. They should offer choice in terms of mobility and access to different activities, buildings and resources. They should not just be wholly oriented towards the particular needs of motorists. Nor, indeed, should they be restricted to the needs of any other individual sector of society.

Towns and cities are about *human contact*. One of the principal reasons why town centres are important to us is that they provide opportunities to bump into people. That means how we get there is important. So is the arrival point. When we get into the centre, there must be suitable places to meet or congregate, which are obvious and easy to find.

Somehow we have got to reduce the impact of motor vehicles. As discussed in the previous chapter,

they are getting everywhere and, quite simply, they are killing our towns and cities. The arrival point – whether an airport, railway station, bus station, multi-storey car park or footpath/pedestrian gateway – must be attractive, friendly and welcoming. The arrival point forms our first impression of a place. The multi-storey car park, for example, must be one of the most unpleasant and unsocial points of arrival in a town or city centre. Many public transport termini are not a lot better.

People and visitors want variety and choice; they want things to do; things to look at; places to go; things to buy; value for money and friendly local people. Citizens want the chance to meet each other. Visitors and tourists look for some quality of *escapism* – places to see and things to do that are different from their normal style of living and working. While catering for this wide range of needs, each town or city must strive to retain its individual, unique character.

Twenty-four-hour access to urban areas is important. How a city looks and works at night or during the week-end will matter a lot to those using it and will determine the nature of its use. Closed-

Few cities have such memorable meeting places as Rome's Spanish Steps, but better multi-storey car parks – like these in Winchester and Woking, England – would transform the usually depressing experience of arriving by car in most towns and cities.

off shopping malls kill urban areas at night-time and weekends. In my opinion, the tendency to try to privatize bits of the urban fabric is a most unfortunate and unhealthy trend.

Access may be inhibited in various ways. Some central areas are, for example, beset by problems of anti-social behaviour – including drug and alcohol abuse. Whilst there may be some physical measures that can be taken to deter miscreants from colonizing parts of the town centre, social and economic solutions need to be found for what are essentially social and economic problems. Some urban authorities, goaded by aggressive Chambers of Commerce, have succeeded in obtaining powers to ban the drinking of alcohol in defined public areas. It is not enough, however, just to drive the problem elsewhere. However distressing it is to see homeless people in our larger cities sleeping and begging in shop doorways, it is no solution, whatsoever, to sweep them away with high pressure hoses.

As discussed in the previous chapter, in many cities it has become difficult, if not impossible, to walk around safely and comfortably. Walls, barriers, underpasses, bridges and steps have confused and complicated streets and pavements which were once easy to traverse. Most town centre ring roads, relief roads or even access roads, whilst being efficient carriers of vehicular traffic are often, to pedestrians, major barriers, all too often enclosed by walls and railings. The aim, as opportunities for change occur, should be to create a *barrier-free* urban area – one where people can easily see and get to where they want to go and where a person pushing a pram or obliged to use crutches or a wheelchair can get around as easily as everyone else. New development should be designed to encourage access and movement in the adjacent streets and spaces. The opportunity should always be taken to remove barriers and open up the town or city to greater accessibility and pedestrian freedom when new development occurs.

The Commission of the European Communities' *Green Paper on the Urban Environment* rightly asserts that the nature of towns and cities should be primarily the concern of those who live and work there, whose co-operation and participation is needed for the successful implementation of any urban policies:

The recent tendency to privatize urban space must be vigorously resisted. One of the world's previously most private places – Beijing's Forbidden City – is now a welcome focus for visitors from all over the world, and the city is richer and more enjoyable as a result.

These urban actors – inhabitants, shopkeepers, consumers, manufacturers, trade groupings – contribute to urban deterioration, but they also suffer its effects and benefit from improvements.

It is, then, in the interests of the community as a whole to encourage and facilitate shared thinking amongst these various players – both within each city and between cities – to exchange ideas, information and examples of best practice.

Thus the community must always be consulted about, and have an involvement in, development projects which will affect it. People need to have a say in the design of the physical environment in which they live, work, shop and play. All too often consultation exercises are a sham or a token to democracy and are carried out after the principal decisions have been made. To be effective and useful, the consultation process should begin early on in the life of a particular project. That way the results will inform the design before ideas become too fixed and intractable. That way the end product is the more likely to please. The trick is to *communicate* – to communicate what the objectives are; to communicate what the range of possibilities

is; to be clear about constraints; to find out what the local needs and aspirations are, but not to give the impression that everything is possible for the asking. Above all, openness and honesty are required.

Architecture and urban design are creative art forms. The design process requires a high degree of creative excellence and originality and this must be allowed for and encouraged to the full. However, unlike such art forms as painting, sculpture, music and literature, the users and perceivers of architecture and urban design cannot exercise the same choice in what they experience. You cannot, unfortunately, turn off an ugly building or one that just doesn't appeal to you, nor can you send it back to the library! This does place an enormous additional burden on the architect and urban designer. It simply isn't possible to say 'I am an artist. I can do what I like. Take it or leave it'. Architects and urban designers must recognize that they have a responsibility to a wider patronage than an individual client. This message should, in my view, be sounded loudly and clearly throughout the architect's educational and professional training.

Recommendations/action checklist

1   Most towns are made to work primarily for the motorist. That should *not* be the priority. Instead, they must be made to work for the pedestrian, the cyclist, the old or disabled person and the school child.

2   Consider carefully how different people will arrive in the town or city centre. Is it an enjoyable experience? How can it be improved?

3   The form of the town should welcome visitors and encourage contact. Are there obvious places where it is easy to congregate and meet people?

4   What are the barriers to access – both physical and social – and how can these be eliminated?

5   Never forget that architecture is the most public of the creative arts.

6   It is essential to consult people early, before plans are prepared and finalized, about potential changes which are going to affect the quality of their environment and their life-style.

Francis Tibbalds Melbourne 1990.

8

Making it Clear

As a man is, so he sees.

William Blake

Different places mean different things to different people. We probably all perceive our urban environment in slightly different ways. What matters is to put together buildings and bits of towns in ways that are easy to understand. The design process should both capture the spirit and character of a place or building in a relevant manner and also seek to articulate these ideas and images in a well-thought-out approach to physical form, materials, colour and design references, which are easily recognized and understood.

Good urban areas are *legible* – they can be understood or read like a book. All this really means in this context is that it should be easy for people, as pedestrians or drivers, to understand where they are, how the town is arranged and which way to go for the different places, amenities and facilities that they require – more simply a legible place is one in which your mother can go shopping and not become confused and lost!

New development needs to have this quality of *legibility*. Linked sequences of spaces help, together with particular landmarks. The skyline may also indicate particular activities (churches, recreation and entertainment buildings) or a concentration of uses (like a cluster of office towers signalling the business centre). An intricate low roofline combined with a complex small-scale street pattern may well signal the historic core of a town or city centre.

Individual buildings can contribute too – especially if they are memorable, useful markers in the townscape. It should be obvious from outside a building what its function is and how to enter it. Conversely, the quality of legibility is hard to achieve in covered, enclosed spaces such as shopping malls and subways and the designer then resorts to extensive signage, which is often both confusing and intrusive.

Some towns and cities are easier to comprehend than others. The more they have been redeveloped the more confusing they tend to be, especially to the visitor. Ways need to be found to make towns and cities, through their buildings and public spaces, more legible. To achieve this the built form needs to be structured in a clear manner – with transport nodes (car parks, rail and bus stations) acting as gateways into the city centre, clear movement systems (for drivers and pedestrian) around the centre,

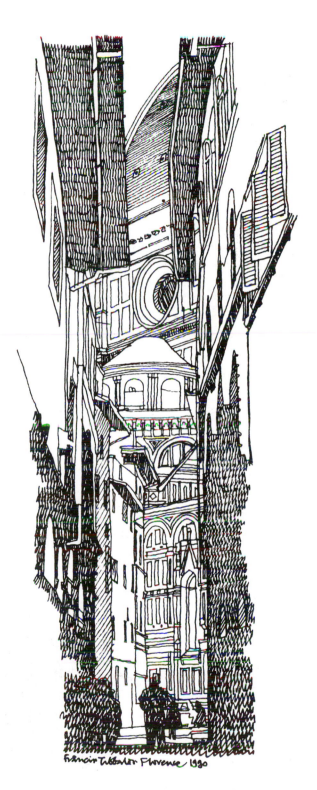

Francis Tibbalds Florence 1990

Even rather undistinguished high buildings, like Melbourne's Rialto Towers marking the south-east corner of the central area, can be useful and effective landmarks. In Florence, multiple linkages and landmarks like the great Duomo help to structure a rich, clear and memorable city centre.

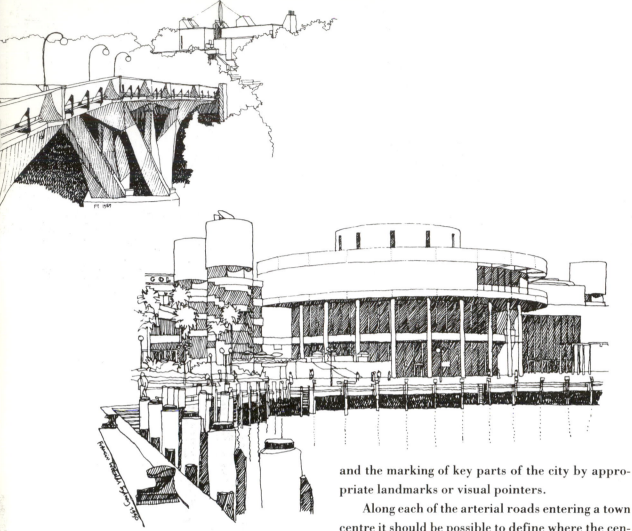

The presence of water in a city should be celebrated, not hidden – open up the waterfront, as at Sydney's Darling Harbour and Liverpool's Albert Dock; make the bridge to the university campus obvious and interesting, as at Peterborough, Ontario, and, exploit to the full the exhilarating opportunities for water, light and a striking building to combine, as at Sydney Opera House.

and the marking of key parts of the city by appropriate landmarks or visual pointers.

Along each of the arterial roads entering a town centre it should be possible to define where the centre begins or should begin. This may be no more than a roundabout or road junction. It may be a significant change of use or bulk and height of buildings. All too often it is nothing – a blurred transition from suburbia or inner city areas to the central area, with a proliferation of derelict sites and ugly advertising hoardings. Once identified, it is possible to emphasize the importance of the entry point – by the form of the adjacent buildings, by the devising of memorable landmarks or by using landscaped open space to maintain a clear break between the centre and the outer urban area.

The actual arrival point in a town or city – be it bus station, railway station or car park – also needs careful attention in terms of its location, its connection to the rest of the central area and the clarity with which these relationships can be understood by the visitor, without reference to maps and signposts. Above all each should celebrate arrival in the particular town or city in which it is located – not an

anywhere car park or public transport terminus in an *anywhere* urban area, but places which tell you clearly and welcomingly that you have now arrived in a specific and recognizable town or city. This can be achieved through the design and layout of the buildings comprising the arrival point – clearly defined entrances and exits and decor related to its local context – and through views and vistas of the surrounding urban fabric, to aid pedestrian orientation.

For those towns with rivers or canals running through their central areas, a wonderful aid to clarity and legibility is presented. Crossing the river in London, Paris or Rome leaves the visitor in little doubt where he or she is. Yet all too often urban rivers and canals are neglected and the potential is wasted – buildings and activities turn their backs on the water, it is hidden from view and the experience of crossing the water is marred by poor bridge design. Waterside land, when it becomes available, is frequently simply covered with commercial uses like offices and hotels. Planning authorities should safeguard defined strips alongside the water's edge for towpaths and promenades linked to the town's

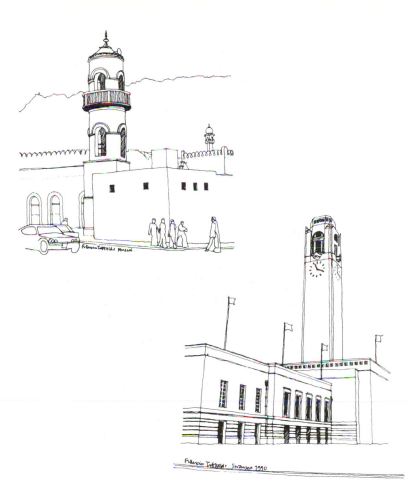

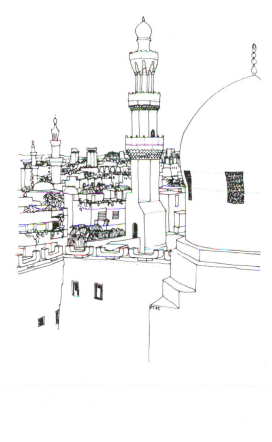

pedestrian network. The objective should be to use the water as a key structuring element to the central area, to let people know that it is there, to facilitate views of it and from it, to line it with appropriate uses and, generally, to exploit its visual and functional potential to the full.

It is often at night that central areas become particularly difficult to comprehend. Uncertainty about where one is and where to go next breeds unease, if not actual fear for one's safety. Key routes and public places need to be well lit and, where practicable, lined with uses that operate after dark. The night-time appearance of central areas can be dramatically enhanced by the imaginative lighting of buildings, streets, trees, sculptures, monuments and public spaces. Major buildings – public buildings, prominent new buildings, richly detailed historic buildings and transport facilities – should be floodlit to create an attractive night-time vitality. The presence of plenty of people going about their business and enjoying themselves is a powerful deterrent to those bent on crime and vandalism. It should also be remembered that water and light together make for the most scintillating, memorable

and magical night-time appearance – whether it be the twinkling canals of Amsterdam or the breath-takingly illuminated sails of the Opera House in Sydney Harbour.

Views and vistas towards interesting, memorable buildings or features are important in assisting orientation – especially for visitors. They also contribute to the image people form of a place and the image that they take away with them. All towns and cities have some worthy buildings and usually some topographical features that provide attractive views. These need to be protected and enhanced, particularly where they are seen from major pedestrian or vehicular traffic corridors.

Tall buildings should be located deliberately – not through arbitrary land economics. They should provide a positive outline to the skyline and mark a particular place or places in the urban fabric – such as the commercial centre. Planning policies of the 1960s and 1970s encouraged the scattering, rather than concentration of high buildings, and this has left many towns and cities with unattractive, anonymous skylines. Tall buildings should not be located where they harm an existing townscape of merit –

Over the centuries, tall buildings have been symbols of religious, governmental or financial power – minarets from Muscat, Oman and Cairo, Egypt; the clock tower of the Civic Centre in Swansea, Wales; the famous towers of San Gimignano, Italy and the distinctive round hotel tower at the heart of downtown Atlanta, Georgia.

Telecommunication towers are useful modern landmarks now constructed in many cities of the world – typical examples from Berlin, Sydney, Toronto and London. The profiles of high buildings are important and they need proper tops (as well as bottoms). Melbourne's Herald Tribune 'lookalike' is memorable, as is the rich 1905 tiled gable spotted in the centre of Belfast, Northern Ireland. The collage of rooftops from Bromley town centre in England, provides an exemplar of the sort of clock towers, cupolas and turrets which traditionally have marked civic buildings on the skyline so effectively and attractively.

such as a heritage or conservation area. Ideally they should be located where they mark a gateway or terminate a key view. They should only be located where they do not adversely affect the local environment in terms of overshadowing, overlooking or wind turbulence – residential areas are particularly sensitive and vulnerable. Tall buildings are very prominent. Their design therefore needs to be of the highest architectural quality in form and detail, with clear profiles, proper tops and proper bottoms.

The strongest image of many towns and cities is provided by the way they relate to physical features, such as hills, rivers and valleys. Where urban areas have such a strong, interesting and clear topographical form it is important that it should not be lost or blurred. In the process of much post-war redevelopment, existing topography has often been ignored or buried by imposing artificial levels – decks, bridges and subways – and an insensitive built form – unrelated to the ground plane and blocking views.

Public and civic buildings should be located to structure the town or city centre, to form memorable parts of the centre and to provide landmarks at the end of key view corridors.

City centres need roads. They also need buildings. But roads and buildings must not become barriers to views or pedestrian movement. It is particularly important to make it easier for pedestrians to find their way around, without resort to extensive signage – however well designed. A city centre's buildings can – by their form, colour and materials – help people to know where they are and where to go for the different facilities and amenities that they want. Different parts, or quarters, of a town or city centre should have distinctive characters. In many towns and cities there may be scope for the definition of new areas or quarters of special character – such as a legal quarter, a Chinese quarter or an area associated with a particular trade or product. The outsides of buildings should be designed to help people recognize what the building is for, what goes on inside and how to enter it.

Most town centres have some topographical interest. Traditionally, the builders of towns and cities have known how to exploit topography to the benefit of the town. In recent development, all too often, natural ground forms and slopes are hidden or covered by decks and platforms. It is much to be

The city of Florence has exploited its natural topography to provide one of the world's great public viewing arenas – the Piazzale Michelangelo, across the River Arno from a breathtaking, distinctive and coherent aerial view of the red Florentine rooftops, above which rises the great cathedral dome by Brunelleschi.

Boulogne, France; Liverpool Pierhead and Oxford city centre, England; Radda in Chianti and San Marino, Italy; and San Francisco, California – topography should be exploited and rooflines deliberately planned.

preferred that buildings should sit upon the real ground and should be arranged to emphasize, rather than hide, a city's natural land form. With few exceptions, it is wrong to put people as drivers into ugly tunnels under buildings. Equally, it will usually be quite wrong to put people as pedestrians on ugly bridges and windy decks up in the air. Topographical variations should be exploited in terms of locating key buildings. Central areas should be structured according to a framework of short and long distance view corridors. The best and most memorable streets are usually those with a closed vista – aligned on a distinctive landmark. Where opportunities exist to create gateways into the central area or special precincts therein, they should be grasped. In many towns and cities it can be an interesting – and maybe breathtaking – experience to see the central area from above. Topography may permit a natural viewing location, such as the Piazzale Michelangelo in Florence. Church towers and other high buildings provide manmade facilities, which are secondary to the main use. In some cities – Paris, Toronto, Sydney and Hong Kong, amongst others – tailor-made facilities have been erected to provide viewing facilities.

New development in our towns and cities needs to be more sensitive, more friendly. We do not want anonymous, hostile *megalumps*. There is room for a lot more fun. Single-use buildings on large blocks need to be avoided at all costs and opportunities grasped to enrich the public realm by extending it, where possible, into the ground levels of buildings on all four sides. As a corollary, adjacent uses should contribute to the vitality and enjoyment of the street. Colour, pattern, decoration, texture, rich materials – as well as technical excellence and innovation – must combine to make buildings that are actually enjoyable for ordinary people to use and look at. Good landscaping, whether hard and formal or soft and informal, is also vital. It always has a softening, mellowing and humanizing effect – knitting together the built fabric to make a coherent, attractive, organic whole.

Finally, one should not ignore the importance of roofscape. The roof is an important fifth elevation, both to an individual building and to urban development overall. Its appearance is important, both intrinsically and as a useful structuring device to aid orientation and memorability. Roofscape design

should never be left as something accidental, unconsidered or unimportant. It must be properly designed and planning authorities should insist on this. In particular the roof should never be just the place where all manner of ugly plant and equipment are deposited in the belief, usually wholly mistaken, that it will never be seen.

Recommendations/action checklist

1 The test of the layout of a town or city centre is how well, or how badly, the visitor can find his or her way at first encounter.

2 Are there clear arrival points?

3 Has the most been made of gateways, landmarks, topographical variation, the night-time appearance and the definition of areas of different character?

4 Is there a clear structure of vistas or view corridors?

5 Are tall buildings well located and do they have distinctive profiles and tops?

6 If a visitor wants to look at the town from above, is there somewhere from which this can be done?

7 Applications for planning permission should not

be entertained unless accompanied by clear evidence that the roofscape has been properly designed.

Roofscape needs to be designed to be seen as a 'fifth elevation'. It can also accommodate functions like terraces, patios and gardens – examples from Quebec, Canada; Florence, Italy; and York, England.

Francis Tibbalds Kings College London 1990

9

Lasting Environments

The bitterness of poor quality is remembered long after the sweetness of the cheapest price is forgotten.

Anon

Short-term expediency can be very harmful to the urban environment. The decisions made during the design and construction of a building project – on the use of resources, the choice of construction materials and the use of energy – can have a long-lasting impact, on the building as a whole and the wider environment. We have become too accustomed to build cheaply and wastefully, to build for immediate effect and to forget that, unlike a landscape which will mature over time, a building, unless well cared for, will do the exact opposite – it will deteriorate. Traditional buildings have lasted for centuries. Today it is unremarkable for a building to be demolished and redeveloped within twenty or twenty-five years, once the developer has got an adequate return on his investment. The cheapness and inflexibility of the original structure often precludes the option of refurbishment as a means of extending the building's life.

There is a better way. Energy and environmental issues should, therefore, be addressed at appropriate levels of the planning and architectural process. All projects should, wherever and whenever possible, be based upon design and technology which is energy-efficient – in terms of performance – and ecologically sound in the short, medium and long terms. Everyone can contribute, no matter how modestly, to the development and enhancement of a sustainable environment.

We must not continue to ignore the time factor in urban development. We are not just building for today. Buildings need to be *robust*. Traditionally, buildings in successful urban areas have had a remarkable ability to adapt over time to changed circumstances and different uses and opportunities. Places which can be used for a variety of purposes offer their users more choice than places whose design limits them to a single fixed use. Places, as a whole, also need to have the quality of robustness. In England, the Georgian town building is the most obvious example of a form of building which has proved particularly flexible in this respect both individually, in its suitability to be used in combination to form whole streets, squares and crescents and in its ability to accommodate different uses over time.

Great consideration should be given to the materials used to construct buildings and development projects. In selecting materials, careful account

Places and buildings need to be robust – built not only to last, but also to adapt to changing needs. These are qualities found in English collegiate architecture, like these examples of King's College London and Trinity College, Cambridge. The 1810 plan of Bath, also in England, remains intact today, although some of the uses of the buildings have changed.

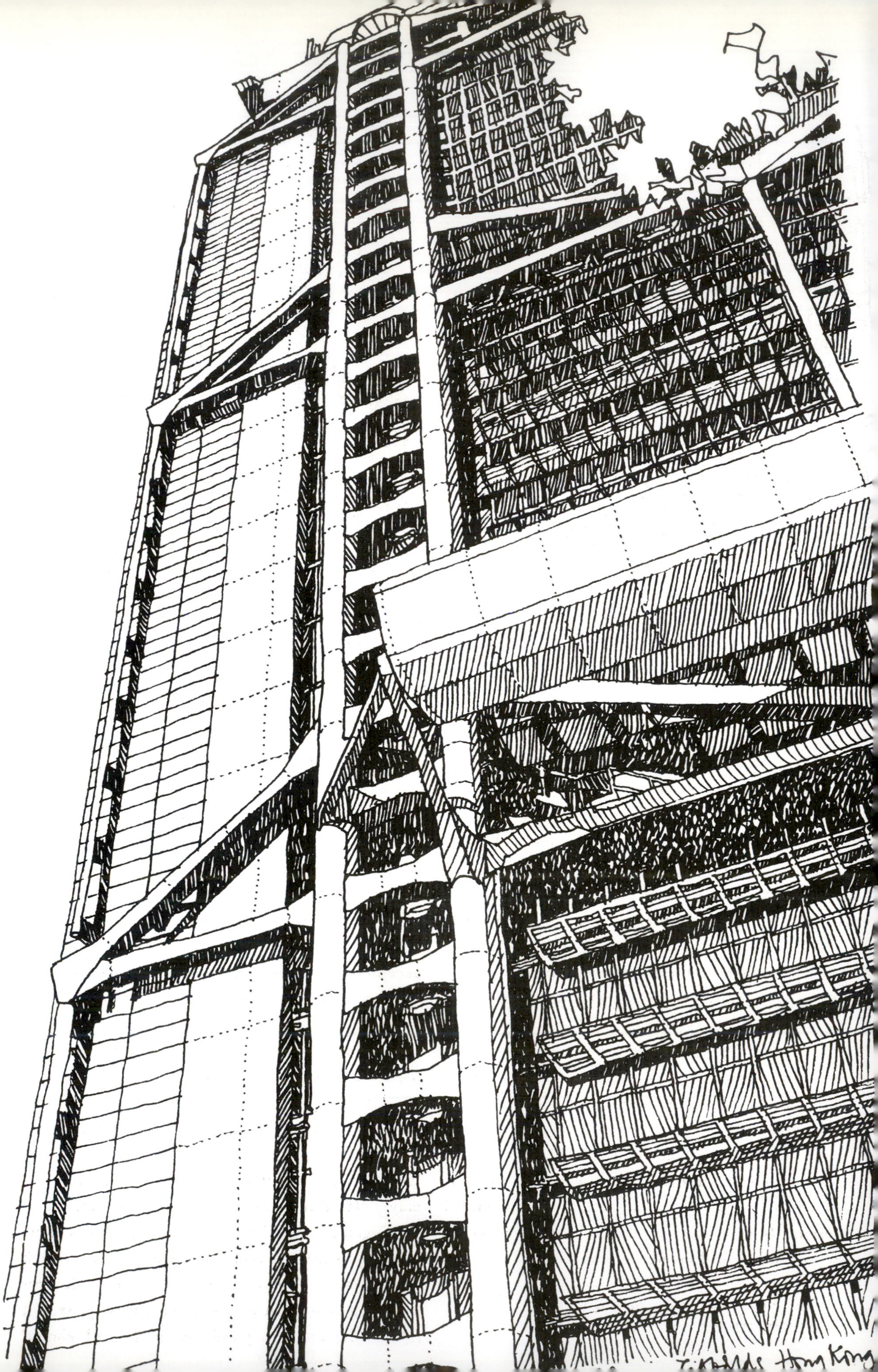

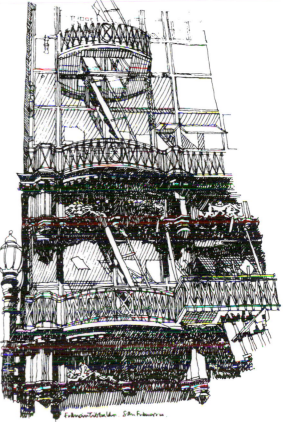

must be taken, amongst other things, of location, scale, neighbouring materials, cost and durability.

If we are prudent we will take care to establish, in early sketches and cost plans, the use of high quality materials. These must remain functionally appropriate and visually pleasing over time. They must cope with the ravages of the weather, consistent with the design life of the particular project. The materials of which our buildings are built need to be selected for their permanence, durability, mellowing and enduring qualities as well as for ease of maintenance.

There is, however, a view, which I have never understood, that the use of good materials will somehow make a poor or mediocre development acceptable. I have never been a lover of the massive Canary Wharf development in London's Isle of Dogs: I object to it for strategic planning and urban design reasons as well as for its shear banality, in my view, as a piece of late twentieth century architectural design. Interviewed by a television reporter in September 1990, I faced the rebuttal:

But, Mr Tibbalds, they've covered it in expensive marble!

As though that could possibly excuse all the deficiencies of which I had been complaining!

Good design and designing for longevity is not, then, about marble and granite entrances or stone fronts and cheap brick backs. It is about choosing the appropriate materials for the location and thinking through the problems of after-care. It is not simply a matter of the most expensive automatically being the best although, of course, it has to be accepted that good quality, long-lasting materials will cost more than less robust, cheap-jack substitutes.

Developers traditionally prefer to spend money where it shows. Unfortunately, their definition of what shows can often tend to be a rather limited one. Hence so many developments exhibit the lavish entrance hall and posh front facade syndrome. Wander round the other side of the building and you may well find an ugly car park, ill-kempt bits of landscaping, unscreened refuse bins; gaping holes in the building to accommodate service bays and car park entrances, surface ducting, ventilation equipment and all manner of other visually intrusive junk. Yet this is still part of the public realm. The rule should

Robustness can be achieved through the use not only of such obviously durable materials as stone – used for cathedrals, like this example from Le Mans, France – and brick – as in these solid Dutch warehouses recently refurbished as residential accommodation – but also iron, steel and glass, depicted in historic examples from The Hague, the Netherlands and San Francisco, United States, and the more recent Hongkong and Shanghai Bank HQ on Hong Kong Island.

Robustness is also needed in the detailing and decoration of building elements. Georgian doorways, windows and balconies; traditional Chinese painted timber roof construction; a modern vehicular entrance; and, an English residential vernacular projecting window provide examples from different countries and different centuries.

be that the building developer can be given considerable design discretion in designing the purely internal, *private* realm. If residents or tenants don't like what has been done, they will find financial or other ways to express their displeasure or dissatisfaction. The *public* realm is an entirely different matter. Here there is an absolute obligation on the developer to consider a wider public who at different times will see or be exposed to the external qualities of the particular buildings.

Lack of maintenance, or poor maintenance in the public realm can also significantly harm perceptions of a place. Street furniture and paving materials must be chosen for their robust, enduring qualities, but they must also be looked after. A brick paved street must not be patched with asphalt. Knocked-down bollards should be quickly reerected. Graffiti must be quickly cleaned off or painted out. Confusing arrays of street furniture, signposting and paving, probably installed by a number of different authorities at different times, need to be sorted out by a single agency.

In the design of streetscape, it is important to avoid trendy styles that date quickly. It is also well

worthwhile trying to integrate functions – so that bollards can act as traffic barriers and cycle stands; lamp-posts can carry signs, flags, hanging plant baskets and so on. Thus, it is perfectly possible to avoid the visually chaotic proliferation of signs and poles that clutter up most urban areas.

Creating lasting environments also means taking a responsible attitude to our heritage. Existing buildings and the activities that they house are a resource: they should not be thrown away lightly. Once gone, they are gone for ever. Particular priority needs to be given to saving small-scale, special, local uses, which are inevitably squeezed out in development schemes, because it is often from these that the particular character of a town or city derives. If they are allowed to be extinguished, the town simply becomes just like any other.

Most towns and cities have lost at least part of their architectural and historic heritage. Some buildings, if not completely lost, are emasculated by facadism – new development behind a retained facade. Once buildings have gone, they cannot be put back. Future generations will not forgive decision-makers who continue to throw away the

heritage of the town or city for expediency or short-term commercial advantages. No historic building should ever be demolished without very sound reason and whatever replaces it must be of a higher design quality.

Recommendations/action checklist

1 What is the design life of the project? Should it not be 50 to 100 years rather than 20 to 30?
2 Will the building(s) accommodate future changes of use?
3 What are the proposals for short and long term maintenance?
4 Think long and hard before demolishing existing buildings. Could they have a longer, useful life?
5 Is the development energy efficient and ecologically sound?
6 Has the developer provided frontages to the public realm which are appropriate, long lasting and attractive? Has the front and back syndrome been avoided in design and choice of materials?
7 Is there a maintenance force to deal quickly with litter, graffiti, broken paving slabs and other

minor, but cumulatively extremely deleterious, damage to the public realm?

The suk buildings of Yanbu on the Saudi Arabian coast of the Red Sea, made of coral blocks and timber, are still in one piece (just). London's Covent Garden Market Hall has been successfully recycled as a speciality shopping centre. Perhaps Toronto's Eaton Centre will be one of the few modern shopping centres to survive the 50 to 100 year test?

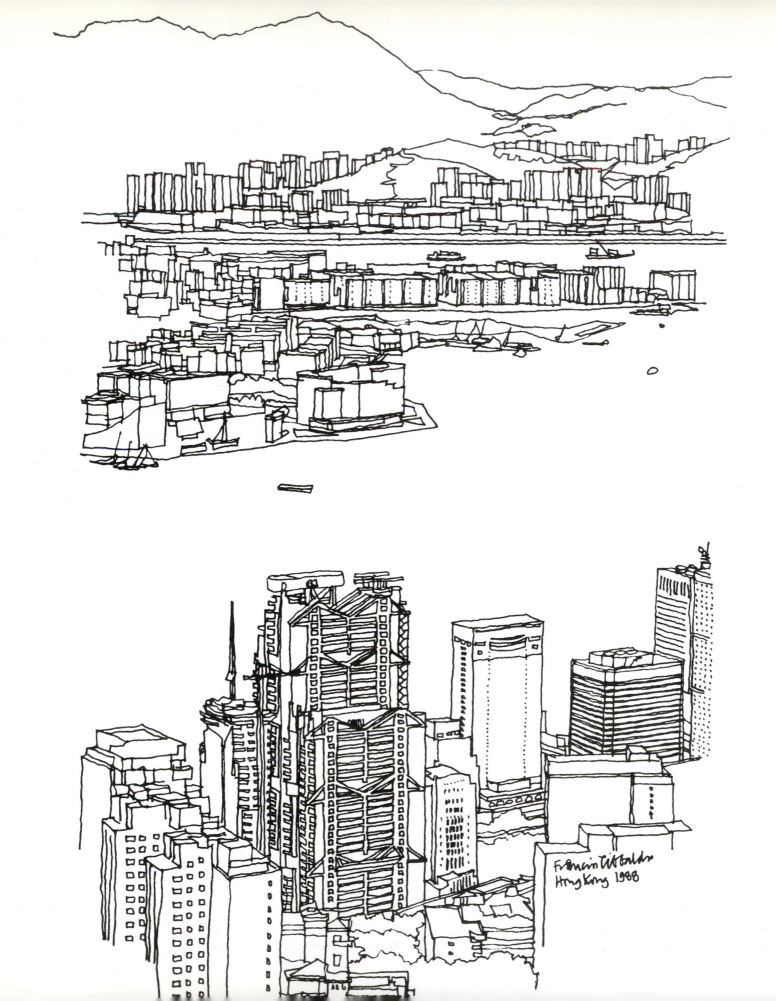

Francis Tibbalds
Hong Kong 1988

10
Controlling Change

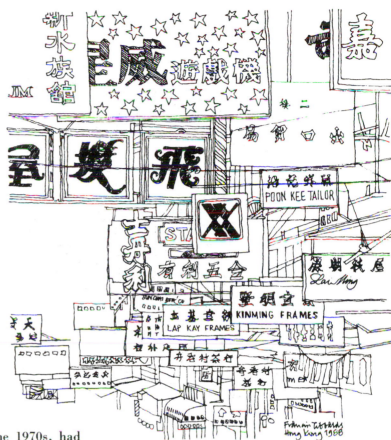

Change is inevitable – but in places where all old buildings have been swept away people feel a sense of insecurity and the continuity is lost for ever. It is essential to keep some buildings of historic or architectural interest of all kinds and all periods – houses, windmills, warehouses, theatres, churches and even some railway stations, most of which can be converted to a modern use, whilst giving visual pleasure to visitors, residents or passers-by.

How Do You Want to Live? 1972

Our towns and cities are, by their very nature, always in a state of flux or change. They are dynamic, rather than static, constructs and the process of design and management must recognize this. We must appreciate, however, that, for most people, *change* involving the loss of familiar surroundings is very painful – particularly so when it occurs on a large or comprehensive scale. So urban change is inevitably a painful process and those involved in it need to recognize this and do everything practicable to minimize or mitigate its harmful impacts. The change will be even worse if it is unexpected, so it is vitally important that the community is fully aware of what is happening, when and why.

The immediate post-war period saw, in many countries, the complete redevelopment of town centres in order to facilitate new social and commercial demands and pressures. The period saw change on an unprecedented scale, often through what might be described as brute force planning and implementation. This produced townscapes which did not always meet with public approval. The devastation of many town centres and their communities led in the 1970s and 1980s to a new movement – the con-

servation lobby. People had, by the 1970s, had enough of brutal change and wanted to keep familiar environments intact.

The issues, as always, are not black and white. It is rarely the case that total preservation is completely right and that total redevelopment is completely wrong. Rather, it is a matter of balance – getting the best of both worlds. Mixing the new and unfamiliar with the old and familiar will usually result in attractive, rich, urban environments which people will find comfortable and enjoyable. If it doesn't all happen too quickly, it will normally be more acceptable.

Historically, urban areas have grown and changed slowly and organically. To the extent that modern day development can be achieved incrementally – healing or mending the edges as it goes – the more acceptable it is likely to be found. We should seek ways to ameliorate the pain of change by the promotion of incremental development. Blood transfusions, rather than organ transplants, are required. What is finding greater favour with the community, as well as developers and their advisers, is an approach characterized by a more contextual,

Hong Kong is a breathtaking modern city which, sadly, is fast eradicating its traditional truly Chinese townscape. The trick is to preserve the best of both worlds.

All over the world, architectural heritage is being destroyed by mindless commercialism – even in Nizwa in the Sultanate of Oman. It is also being devalued by equally mindless pastiche – modern-day imitation of past styles – as here in the expensive Shenzhen Hotel near the Peoples' Republic of China's border with Hong Kong.

organic, incremental and sensitive way of thinking and designing. We need, then, to encourage the development of smaller sites, set limits on the extent of site assembly and break up the larger sites into more manageable components.

So-called comprehensive redevelopment schemes have devastated many towns and cities. Many cities appear to have had more than their fair share. On the other side of the world, the rich Victorian city of Melbourne has suffered almost irreparable damage in the past five years from the State Premier's desire to have '*more cranes on the skyline*'. In the 1950s and 1960s, the centre of Birmingham – England's second city – underwent change on an unprecedented scale, in terms of new built development and the construction of roads and multi-storey car parks. Whilst this resulted in considerable commercial vitality and an almost unique level of accessibility for motorized vehicles, it also produced a physical environment that now falls short of public aspirations. It is vital that other places avoid such mistakes – they are very difficult to repair or correct.

It is depressing to see how so-called progress has wreaked so much damage upon so many towns and cities. As succinctly pointed out in *How Do You Want to Live?*:

A huge slab block which might look reasonable in Brasilia or set against the hills of Hong Kong can look totally incongruous towering over attractive Edwardian buildings at Mancastle on Trent. Or a supermarket which would be unnoticed in the outskirts of Los Angeles, can totally destroy the scale of the Georgian cottages at Little-Puddleton-in-the-Marsh....We have seen a block of flats in Wales built on a high ridge which dominates the town, when a lower site would have been visually acceptable, but doubtless more difficult for the architect and more expensive for the developer. New hotels in London too numerous to mention, have destroyed squares and shattered whole areas of low scale residential streets by their huge bulk. In other cities the centre has often been gutted to provide sites for concrete offices or large shopping precincts beside which the Victorian Town Hall, or the Georgian Art Gallery, left behind as a sop to tradition, look alienated and completely out of place.

The conservation movement has been no bad thing, in this respect, in that not only has it encouraged the retention of cherished buildings and areas, but also it has fostered the development of new skills in sensitive infilling. The pity is that it was largely a reaction to the fear that new invariably equals worse.

Conservation implies, not preservation for the sake of it, but the retention and enhancement of all

that is good in an area – not just in a historical or architectural sense, but in terms of providing a setting for normal vigorous urban life. The challenge, as recognized by Colin Buchanan and Partners in their *Conservation Study of Bath*, is to find new uses for empty and decaying buildings, to deal with the adverse effects of traffic and to bring the area back to life.

We need to sweep away the confusion and clutter that make so many places so similar and so unattractive, but not to harm the good bits in the process. Good maintenance is, as discussed in the previous chapter, every bit as important as good design. Many existing buildings present an unattractive or neglected appearance. This does not necessarily mean that they have to be pulled down. In many instances, upgrading the existing built environment is the more sensible option and the better value for money.

Change, then, need not be about wholesale redevelopment: it can be about a process of gradual improvement and sensitive facelift schemes, which, taken as a whole, can have a dramatic effect on the quality and appearance of an area. Such schemes

should provide for the upgrading of important facades, the removal of prominent eyesores, the removal of all advertising which is intrusive and/or blocks views, the improvement of shopfronts and street frontage design and the introduction of better, simpler, co-ordinated street furniture. Facade improvement should be extended to prominent, ugly buildings – and, sadly, the majority of multi-storey car parks come into this category. Measures available to a local public authority to achieve such schemes should include grant-aiding facade improvements (possibly with a pump-priming scheme for priorities), facade cleaning grants, the encouragement of street owner groups, promulgation of good practice and the fostering of award schemes by civic and amenity societies.

Large-scale advertising hoardings should generally be discouraged, except where they are used to screen ugly buildings, to screen major infrastructural works or to relieve blank facades, where they are designed as an integral part of a building. On building site hoardings the opportunity can often be successfully taken to introduce temporary art and murals. Smaller advertisements can usually be

Relatively small scale changes – like improvements to shopfronts and signage – should be welcomed.

The refurbished Michelin building in London's South Kensington demonstrates how rich decoration can be successfully recycled.

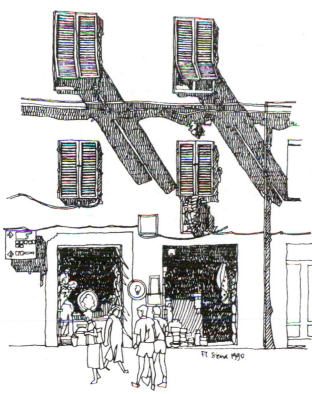

satisfactorily accommodated on well-designed drum and similar units. Illuminated advertising should generally be discouraged, except in such recognized bright lights areas as London's Piccadilly Circus or New York's Broadway. Visitors to Hong Kong Island and Kowloon will, however, readily appreciate that done on a large scale and with uninhibited panache illuminated advertising can become electric architecture of a breath-taking quality.

It is almost axiomatic that every developer of a site will initially seek to erect a greater bulk of floorspace than it will comfortably hold. Even those developers who profess caring attitudes to the environment on public platforms still adopt this tactic. Until better systems are developed for the regulation of land prices and discouragement of speculation by those for whom a site is no more than a vehicle for maximising profits, it is likely that such tactics will not change. Invariably, what is actually built, after negotiation with the appropriate planning authority will still be slightly too big for comfort on the site. Individually, some may argue that this does not matter. But cumulatively it does. The cumulative effect of developments which are all a bit bigger than they

ought to be will have a seriously detrimental effect on the quality and character of a town and planning authorities should guard against this.

Some planning regimes around the world actually exacerbate this situation by permitting extra floorspace – and hence bulk – in return for some public benefit, such as the provision of a paved forecourt or the restoration of an adjoining listed building. However worthy such benefits, if the price is an unacceptably large new building, then, quite simply, the price is too high. Such horse-deals are crude and do not contribute to the overall improved quality of a place. Other ways must be found to fund worthwhile public benefits. In some places such benefits are now required anyway, before permission will be granted for the new development, without any question of allowing it to be even bigger.

It is easy to see the appeal to a single owner, developer or even tenant of a single development occupying a whole street block, rather than a series of individual properties. The same block may be internalized, turning its back on the public realm of the street and omitting the interest and variety provided by doors and shop windows. It does not take

Shopfronts do not need to be vast glazed areas unrelated to the building in which they are set. Sienese ones are modest, yet workable. Whilst the scales are different, Frank Lloyd Wright's entrance to the Morris shop in San Francisco is echoed in Terry Farrell's entrance to the Tobacco Dock speciality shopping centre in London's Docklands. Both entice the customer without banal signage, advertising and window displays.

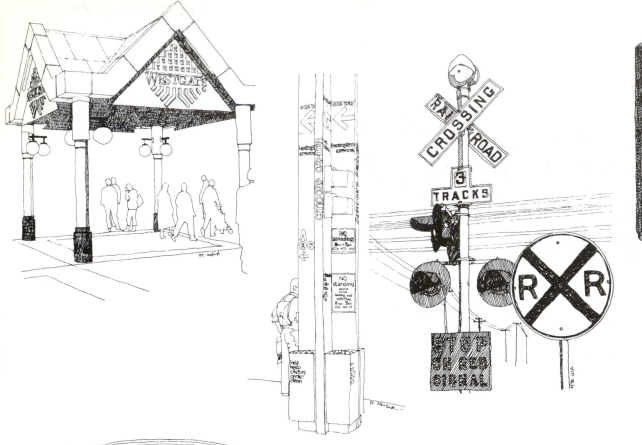

Avoid clutter, redundant signage and the banal standard solution which destroys local individuality. Good street furniture should be appropriate to the place - a modern freestanding canopy in Oxford, a multi-purpose information column by the Citicorp development in New York and an attractive advertising drum from Amsterdam.

more than two or three such developments, especially if they are adjacent to one another, to kill the public street life of a town.

Many developments do not need to be so big and lumpy. Shopping centres are made up of units which are small, medium and large. They do not need to be forced together into one lump, overwhelming the character of the town, destroying the traditional urban grain, presenting bland exteriors and acres of awkwardly joined roofs which are exceedingly ugly when viewed from above. They can be put together in all manner of ways to provide variety of block sizes, intricacy of pedestrian routes, the insertion of other uses, access to other uses at upper level, some covered spaces, some open to the sky – in short, an environment which, without being contrived, is familiar, easy to understand and enjoyable, in the way that traditional centres are. Local communities, through their elected councils, want to improve shopping and other facilities, for their own benefit and for the commercial vitality of the town. But this does not have to be achieved at the price of a rotten new environment. If this is unacceptable to the first developers who comes along, then they should simply

be sent away. If enough authorities had the guts to do this, the poor and mediocre developers, for whom all that matters is quick lettings to ubiquitous chain retailers, will either quickly go out of business or decide to mend their ways.

The same is true of office development. Provided it is well-serviced, has good natural light and views and is reasonably efficient in space planning terms, it can be moulded to all manner of site shapes. It does not need to be rigidly rectilinear – many ugly set-backs and left-over spaces have resulted from imposing a rectangular footprint upon an irregular, non-rectangular site. In general terms, street frontages should be maintained in a manner that is consistent with the grain of the area. It may well stretch the designer's talents to avoid the usual, dead frontage of an office building abutting a public pavement. The argument is not for an applied stage-set facade – for example, respecting old property party walls – which have no real relationship with the building behind. Rather, the base of the building should capitalize on the design opportunities arising from the entrance, the need for public access – including for disabled people, display and exhibition

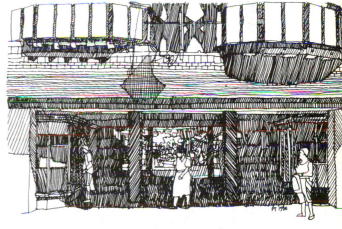

space and showcases relating to the occupants' products or processes. A human-scale exterior is required which clearly communicates *'This is an office building. This is what goes on inside. These are the sorts of people who work here'* – not *'This is private. Go away'*. Clearly, a human-scale exterior will more easily be achievable where the street level accommodates mixed uses and these should always be insisted upon, where realistically achievable, by the planning authority.

Office developers have been accustomed to build high – to secure the prestige of visibility or simply to pile as much accommodation on to a restricted site as possible. Daylighting controls have not always helped the creation of forms of development which are compatible with the local urban grain. For example, the long low slab above which rises a stubby high slab at right angles scraping past the light cones, has proved particularly destructive. Yet high buildings are not the most efficient form of office building. They are expensive to construct and maintain, they are inflexible and they frequently offer a poor ratio between net and gross floorspace. Invariably their design is too coarse, too bland or too bulky. Firm

control needs, therefore, to be exercised over the location of tall office buildings, and their height and design – particularly the profile as expressed by the slenderness ratio and the treatment of the rooftop.

Big development, low risk and quickly constructed, may be convenient in a commercial, business or administrative sense. It is rarely satisfactory in terms of its impact on the public environment of a town or city centre, particularly when it sets a mediocre precedent for others to follow. In the traditional town, the large building – the cathedral, castle, palace, town hall, hospital, college – is an exceptional and noteworthy constituent of the urban fabric, not something to be mindlessly copied.

One of the problems of change is that difficult central sites are left and peripheral sites are redeveloped. This results in the phenomenon of the hollow centre or doughnut, in which the central area gradually dies. It is important not to try to escape the problems of a city or town – particularly the central and inner areas – by extending the periphery. Problems need to be solved within the existing boundaries, not just moved somewhere else.

New office buildings do not need to be bland blocks with flat roofs. New shopping centres do not need to destroy historic towns. Good examples of each are the riverside palace-like Embankment Place, Charing Cross, London and the shopping centre in Salisbury, England, which is entered beneath a fourteenth century building – the Old George Hotel.

Beware too the let-it-all-rip, free-for-all, ebullient, market approach to development. London's Docklands are still paying the price for this approach on the Isle of Dogs and hastily seeking better ways of handling later stages of development. The United Kingdom's greatest urban regeneration opportunity of the century has ended up as a combination of market-led opportunism, architectural chaos and mediocrity. Other places must learn from such mistakes. It will be hard for urban authorities to swallow, but sometimes it will be better for no development to happen, than to permit the wrong development. I can see no evidence that Britain's Enterprise Zone legislation, in which planning controls were lifted and financial incentives offered, has produced environments which have any of the qualities discussed in this book.

In the context of change, tensions occur. There is the obvious tension between the pedestrianization of attractive little streets and the needs of servicing. More complex is the tension between a city trying to retain its heritage while providing modern facilities and amenities. Paris solved this tension by moving the pressure for new development westwards to La Défence – consisting of fairly mediocre megalumps, unrelated to the historic core, other than by its position on the continuation of the grand axis. Chicago, San Francisco and, to some extent, London, work on the basis of co-existence and continual re-adjustment.

There is always a need for small-scale, incremental initiatives. While an overall vision is helpful as a catalyst, as a focus and to create confidence and certainty, often the greatest potential for improving a town or city centre will lie in the co-ordination of relatively minor initiatives and developments which, whilst achieved incrementally, can contribute to a collective whole which is greater than the sum of the individual components.

Recommendations/action checklist

1   Does the site need to be developed in toto? Could at least some of the buildings be refurbished to give richness, complexity and some continuity with the past?

2   Can the site, if large, be broken down into smaller parcels and developed incrementally within an overall framework and without leav-

ing raw edges or producing the impact of a long term building site?

3   It is not axiomatic that comprehensive redevelopment is a good thing. The results of this approach in the past decades have usually been disastrous for towns and cities. Nor is it axiomatic that piecemeal development is a bad thing – because therein often lies the route to more appropriate, sustainable, human scale development.

4   Don't concentrate on easy, peripheral sites and neglect the difficult central ones – for that way the town centre will surely die.

5   Recognize that change is painful to people. Explain what is happening, when and why.

6   The local community will welcome being involved in beneficial change in which it can have a direct and beneficial role, like face-lift schemes and the removal of clutter.

7   Don't barter increased size or floorspace for public benefits that should be provided anyway by a particular development.

8   Avoid being swept along in the hype of a market-led attitude which suggests that development should be accepted at any price.

Francesca Titchmarsh, Siena 1990

11

Joining it all Together

Stones make a wall, walls make a house, houses
make streets, and streets make a city. A city
is stones and a city is people; but it is not
a heap of stones, and it is not just a jostle
of people. In the step from the village to
the city, a new community organisation
is built, based on the division of labour
and on chains of command.

Jacob Bronowski 1973: *The Ascent of Man*

The human animal requires a spatial territory in
which to live that possesses unique features,
surprises, visual oddities, landmarks and
architectural idiosyncracies.

Desmond Morris: *The Human Zoo*

In the preceding nine chapters, nine urban design themes have been separately described. All of them are capable of contributing to the creation of more people-friendly towns and cities. Many of them overlap – pedestrian freedom and human scale are closely related; so are the concepts of mitigating the impact of change and producing a lasting, robust physical environment. In different circumstances, different combinations will emerge as more important than others. If I had to choose two, it would be the need to concentrate on places rather than buildings and the pursuit of mixed uses. What must be recognized is that, because these nine themes are so inextricably related one to another, they work best in combination. And so this last chapter or theme is about just that – *linking them all together*.

The overall objective must be the creation of a rich, vibrant, mixed-use environment, that does not die at night or weekends and is visually stimulating and attractive to residents and visitors alike. We can learn much from what has succeeded in the past, without mindlessly copying it. There is no reason why we cannot develop new urban forms and buildings which have traditional virtues. It isn't necessary to resort to classical pastiche – a cop-out which devalues history – or to the mean graph paper facades of the 1950s and 1960s which have left so many places looking boringly the same.

We should be prepared to use new and innovative ideas and technologies where these are appropriate and they can afford good solutions to development problems, particularly in ways which are more interesting and visually pleasing than more traditional approaches.

We need to be very clear about the context within which we are working. A city's or town's planning strategies need always to address three principal areas of concern:

1   Conserving the best of the past
2   Looking after present needs, and
3   Devising an appropriate future.

The essence of good planning and urban design is to consider all three of these concerns in a balanced and integrated way, for it is when we concentrate on just one, to the exclusion of the others, that problems are likely to arise.

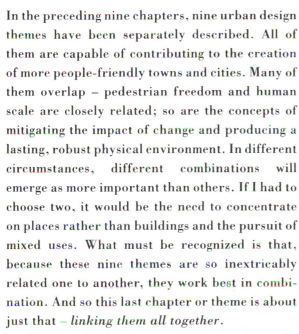

The way all the elements of the urban environment fit together is most important. Siena, for example, has a coherent townscape, with clear routes focused on the city gates. Beyond at least some parts of the city wall, the countryside begins immediately, without any sprawling suburbia. In Windsor, tight-knit English townscape clusters around the royal castle on the hill, to make a coherent whole.

The issues in urban design are never black and white. They are not about extreme choices. They are about balance. It *is* possible to have a high quality, attractive physical environment and good accessibility. It *is* possible to have a lively, human scale central area and commercial prosperity. Above all buildings and development must be appropriate to, and unique to, the particular town or city in which they are located. They must not be a collection of inappropriate transatlantic copies or tired, anonymous solutions that can be seen almost anywhere in the world. People do not want bland, international places: they want places that are unique and special. It is also important not to overlook the importance of how a city looks at night-time.

The centres of towns and cities should generally be medium-rise, mixed use, shopping, business and entertainment areas with any taller buildings carefully located to enhance topographical variations and not to detract from smaller-scale conserved areas. Residential uses should be encouraged wherever practicable and places of civic and historic importance conserved and protected. Much greater emphasis needs to be given to the achievement of a protected and friendly pedestrian environment. Through traffic must be gradually eliminated and traffic calming techniques used to improve the environment of all central area streets.

The city or town centre is for all people. It is not merely for governments, local councils, developers, investors or sectional business interests. The public realm, especially related to people walking about, is what matters most. The quality of the city should not depend upon how it has struggled to accommodate more and more motor vehicles. The perceived form of the city should derive less from individual buildings – however well designed – and more from the major spaces – streets, squares, parks and water – and the combination and clustering of buildings in plan and on the skyline. Keeping town centres bright, clean and attractive contributes a great deal to their success. It attracts customers to the centre – both residents and visitors – and encourages them to want to come back. Traditionally it has often been Municipal Engineers who achieved this, because they had the authority and the resources to achieve improvements on the ground. The need today is for Town Managers to be appointed to take on this function.

St Martin's Lane, in London's West End, is a favourite street. It has a rich mixture of uses, including many entertainment buildings, enormous variety in the age and style of its architecture and a slightly curving alignment in which the distinctive spire of St Martin's in the Fields provides a constant and dramatic landmark at the corner of the tourist Mecca of Trafalgar Square beyond.

Consistency of character can be an asset to a town – whether to a whole town centre, like St Andrews in Scotland, or just one coherent part of the centre, like the developing chinese quarter in Melbourne.

The tension between new and old parts of a town or city must be positively exploited to produce a design environment with a rich and complex association between new and old places. The one must not swamp or shout down the other. New development must be of a high quality and city authorities must turn their backs firmly away from the free enterprize, deregulated model of cities like Houston or Atlanta. Quality and permanence are required, together with the right uses, to produce buildings which are of listable quality in the future, adding in a sensible, incremental way to the heritage of the town or city.

Many towns and cities have a number of distinct quarters, which are of a homogeneous or potentially homogeneous townscape character. Such a character will derive from the uses; the height; the scale and bulk of buildings; colour, materials and texture; topography; edges; roof profiles; landscape; landmarks, and so on. The salient features need to be identified for each area and these must be taken into account in devising development or rehabilitation proposals, with a view to emphasising the uniqueness of not only the town or city, but also each of the constituent parts thereof, underlining the differences from the adjoining ones. But great care is needed.

I'm sure George Melly struck some chords, when he wrote about London in the *Guardian* newspaper in 1989 as follows:

Covent Garden was paved with good intentions. When the flowers and vegetables moved west, and with the perfectly respectable aim of preventing developers from knocking it down, it was transformed into premises for shops, studios, small businesses and restaurants. At least that was the intention. What it eventually became was a camped-up setting for a bowdlerized version of The Beggars Opera.

He also attacked the Chelsea Harbour scheme as '*Fake-believe*' at its most insidious – '*an expensive enclave, well-protected by a paramilitary presence against any possible insurrection*', drawing a parallel with Terry Gilliam's film *Brazil*. He complained at the cobblescaping of Portobello Road as possibly the first stage of its transformation into some kind of 'cockney' theme park.

Nor are buildings all that we need to take account of. Many major European cities enjoy a

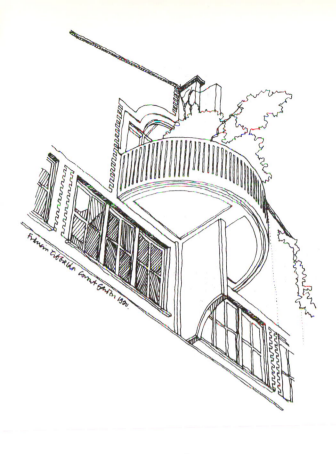

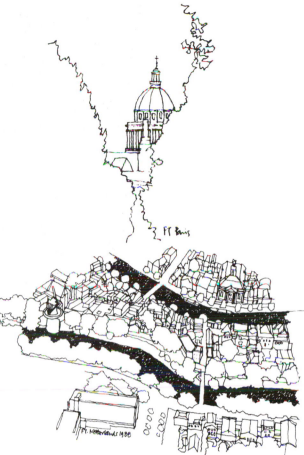

wonderful legacy of urban parks, planted squares and tree-lined boulevards. Other towns and cities have been less fortunate. Green landscaping within towns and cities is important for its visually softening effect and for its contribution to the sustainability and ecological balance of the urban area – it is, for example, now scientifically proven that trees really do act as pollution screens. Wherever possible, new planting should be introduced to mark key pedestrian routes and to provide sheltered havens and that unique quality of dappled sunlight. The landscaping framework can be part of the organizational structure of the city, provided it is well integrated with the built fabric. Thus, it is possible and desirable to locate high density, mixed use, built up areas contiguously with parks and green lungs – they work together.

Open sites and spaces can often be enhanced by tree-planting to re-establish the building line and/or to create more attractive open car parking areas. Even a single tree in the right place can make an enormous contribution to the townscape. It is impossible not to think of the tree in the curving middle portion of Oxford High Street – described by Thomas Sharp as '*the most important tree in the world*'.

As professionals, as administrators and as citizens we need to develop better skills at taking a synoptic view of urban areas. This means taking a comprehensive overview of each area – where it has come from, where it has got to and where it is going. We need to develop better ways of understanding how things fit together to make a whole which is greater than the sum of the individual parts. We also need to understand how certain combinations may produce adverse impacts which can be avoided or mitigated. We underestimate the complexity of the urban environment at our peril. To try to comprehend it and work with it is, by contrast, a deeply rewarding experience.

There is, then, a lot to think about – more than any individual can carry in his or her head at any one time. How, therefore, can we arrive at better processes for deciding whether a development is good or bad? Whether it should be granted permission to proceed or simply be refused? I suggest that there a number of simple questions that can be asked of development proposals to determine whether or

The value of greenness in a city cannot be overstated, whether it takes the form of the mature tree-lined boulevards of Paris and canal-sides of the Netherlands, or visually important single trees – like those in Oxford High Street and a Sienese back street or just a well-planted balcony.

not a development is on the right lines according to the criteria for people-friendly places advanced in this book. They are set out in the recommendations below. Collectively, these could be used by those making decisions about development applications as a checklist to keep by their elbow. Ideally the list should be expanded to include questions of a local relevance or significance to the particular town.

Recommendations/action checklist

1 To encourage more sensitive, friendly developments in which colour, pattern, texture and materials – as well as technical excellence and innovation – combine to create enjoyable places and attractive buildings.

2 To encourage good craftsmanship and after care of buildings and landscape and to recognize the value, where appropriate, of the integration of pieces of art to enrich the public environment.

3 To recognize that, whilst sites must be found for individual set-piece buildings, deliberately located in the townscape, cities are predominantly composed of backcloth buildings which can be manipulated and put together in combination to make a rich and interesting physical urban environment.

4 To prepare development and urban design briefs for key sites.

5 To encourage developers and their architects to look beyond the boundaries of their sites and to prepare three-dimensional material as part of development proposals and pre-application consultations.

To architects, developers and town planners, to ask the following questions:

1 Is the proposed development, by its form, location or use a special/landmark building or a background/backcloth building?

2 Is this judgement agreed by all parties and is it appropriate to the existing and future potential urban design characteristics of the site and environs?

3 Will the development be viewed close to, or at medium or long range, or some combination of these? How will this affect the preferred overall height, roof profile and degree of detail – particularly close to eye level?

Every development proposal should be assessed against explicit planning and urban design criteria to ensure its appropriateness.

4   Should the building be simple or complex?

5   Is the proposed building in the right location, on the right site and/or in the right part or quarter of the city?

6   Does the building accommodate mixed uses or a single use? Can the uses be clearly expressed in the design and is it clear where the front door is?

7   Are there unusable left over bits of site that will be ugly and hard to maintain?

8   Can the development, if on a large scale, be achieved incrementally or organically to avoid the pain of wholesale, rapid change?

9   Does the development help people, as pedestrians and drivers, to know where they are and where to go next?

10   Does the building have a pedestrian-friendly frontage?

11   Does the development encourage ease of pedestrian movement and offer, if appropriate, some degree of protection from bad weather?

12   Will the building be well maintained externally, as well as internally, and how will this affect the choice of materials?

13   What is the likely life of the building? Does this influence short term decisions? Is there a future potential for the site still to be released?

14   What are the predominant colours, materials, patterns and features either existing or proposed in the vicinity of the site? Are these appropriate for the form and use of the proposed building functionally and visually? If not, is it appropriate still to attempt to harmonize with the environs or should there be a deliberate decision to contrast with them?

15   If the site is within a Conservation Area, does the proposal preserve and enhance its character or appearance? Innovative, sensitive design will normally be preferred to pastiche replication of historical styles, if it is demonstrably sympathetic and appropriate to its surroundings.

16   Have all sides of the building, including the roofscape, been considered and designed in relation to the adjacent public realm?

Francis Tibbalds Pompidou Cen

12

A Renaissance of the Public Realm?

*Man is a singular creature. He has a set of gifts which
make him unique among the animals: so that, unlike them,
he is not a figure in the landscape. In body and in mind he is
the explorer of nature, the ubiquitous animal, who did
not find but has made his home in every continent.*

Jacob Bronowski 1973: *The Ascent of Man*

*The most powerful drive in the ascent of man is his pleasure in
his own skill. He loves to do what he does well and, having
done it well, he loves to do it better. You see it in his science.
You see it in the magnificence with which he carves and builds,
the loving care, the gaiety, the effrontery. The monuments
are supposed to commemorate kings and religions, heroes,
dogmas, but in the end the man they commemorate is man
the builder.*

Ibid.

Planning is about determining the future environment and looking after our heritage. Market forces and free enterprise would not give high priority to either of those activities – and why should they? They are primarily concerned with the private rather than the public realm. We have a planning system quite simply because it is difficult for fragmented private interests to care for the public realm – whether that be the provision of a major piece of infrastructure or the protection of a beautiful rural area or a historic town centre, or deciding where is the best place to locate major new development. How can disparate private interests ensure that resources are invested to maximum effect and benefit? There are now dozens of examples of overseas aid programmes where huge investment in capital development has resulted in all manner of white elephants, because nobody thought it necessary to carry out a little planning first – quite ironic, when the cost of this is so negligible when set against construction and implementation costs. Planning, then, can be cost-effective – good value for money.

If we want a vision of what happens with little or no planning – to see the inevitable environments of private affluence and public squalor – there are many places we can go – the Middle East, the United States, many Third World countries (try Lagos for starters!) – and, I dare to ask, is the London Docklands area going the same way? There is an example of a free market environment – are the banal Canary Wharf and surrounding mess of superficial Legoland buildings on the Isle of Dogs really what we want? Fortunately the Royal Docks area may be better as the Development Corporation is now subscribing to a bit more planning and urban design.

By contrast, I have had the fascinating experience of taking a helicopter trip over a large part of Holland. I couldn't have had a more cogent physical demonstration of successful urban planning – clearly defined towns, well-located new settlements, a very comprehensive transport and infrastructure system and a protected Green Heart for agriculture and recreation. It *can* be done. Planning achievements are achieved over long time spans. Short-term cycles in the development market, coupled with the relatively short-term periods of office of central and local governments, do not provide the best context

*Both new buildings and refurbished buildings can
contribute to an enhanced public realm. Fantastic
viewing opportunities are provided from the top of
the Centre Pompidou, Paris, while space for all manner of public outdoor theatre now exists in front of
Covent Garden's remodelled Market Hall.*

for the achievement of long-term visions. A coalition of interests is required, subscribing to an agreed vision and committed to making it happen over a potentially very long time scale. The vision will be multi-faceted and undoubtedly beset by many ifs and buts. Out of the complexity will need to come one or two, key, simple, cogent ideas which are easy to grasp and capture the imagination of the city's administrative, business and residential community. It is vital, particularly at times of recession and a slowing down of development activity, that cities hold out for what is right in the longer term. Compromise, poor quality, 'development at any price' will cause long-lasting damage and quickly be bitterly resented.

Recessions in the construction industry actually provide wonderful opportunities to sort out some of the problems of the past, to take stock of the town or city and decide what is best for its future. It is a chance, not to make imprudent concessions to developers, but to retain low-cost, smaller uses, while preparing for a future up-turn.

There is the need to take a twenty to fifty year view of a city's future: not a three or four year one.

It is vital to look beyond what is politically expedient in the short term. Ideally there should be multi-partisan commitment to explicit strategic goals as a better framework for making business and other decisions about the future of the city. Commitment to good ideas is vital, so that politicians are able to carry forward their implementation beyond three to five year governmental cycles.

Towns and cities can learn from each other. Their inhabitants and administrators need to be ever watchful that they do not make the same mistakes as other cities around the world – particularly *vis à vis* private cars, single-use monolithic development, elevated pedestrian decks and bridges, internal retail malls and a hands-off approach to planning. Mixed uses are important, not just to create an interesting, lively city. Wealth, of ideas as well as capital, is created by putting different disciplines, people and activities, cheek-by-jowl. New ideas are born as they are sparked off one another. There is the need for like-minded people to work in close association with each other, collegiate-style, not in separate organizations or Ministries. They need direct access to decision-makers and those who control the

The skyline of a city is an expression of the public realm, in which culture, commerce, entertainment and living come together for the good of the inhabitants – the skyline of the City of London seen from the west.

New buildings are getting friendlier in their mass and detailing – inventive windows at Robinson College, Cambridge and mellow dockside housing at the new Maritime Quarter in Swansea, Wales. Great care is still needed not to squeeze out marginally economic uses – like this umbrella shop in a side street off London's Charing Cross Road – which, though small, make a disproportionately high contribution to the public life of a city.

city's resources. Strong, single-minded leadership is vital.

The British planning system has actually secured many worthwhile achievements – protection of rural areas, planned growth in urban areas, conservation of our heritage, protection to old buildings, planned new towns and cities, urban regeneration and sensitive re-structuring of existing towns to accommodate new uses, to mitigate the effects of traffic and to create new pedestrian areas. Although, for the most part, it totally failed to stop the devastation wreaked on many town and city centres by the comprehensive redevelopment schemes of the 1950s and 1960s – now hated and reviled by the community and today's professionals – we can all think of dreadful proposals which have been stopped by the British development control system.

As an urban designer, I am less interested in wringing hands about past mistakes by architects and planners – anybody can criticize. What is more important is to cultivate a new spirit of collaboration between architects, planners, developers and the community. Where this is happening, it is bringing a wholly better approach to our work.

In Britain, another favourable sign is the quality of results in fairly run-of-the-mill developments in our towns and cities. Buildings are on the whole friendlier. New buildings are increasingly respecting their context and are developing on a human scale which is concerned with pedestrian comfort and involves areas of mixed land use. I welcome unreservedly today's more humble approach throughout the development professions and the industry. The arrogance of the past made for a lot of friction, but now at least some professionals are listening properly to what people have to say. Even developers and their agents are getting the message. They are generally prepared to go out to public discussion on schemes at an earlier stage than hitherto. They are finding that good design pays. It is popular and good value for money. It matters to some of them that people like what they are producing.

One cannot ignore the profit motive in the stimulation of development and the need for patrons. Even Florence needed its patrons to achieve its superb townscape, in the form of the Church and the great banking families. However, it is quite wrong for buildings or whole towns to be viewed

simply as vehicles for making money for a limited number of people. Architecture and town planning are amongst the most public of the arts – they cannot be switched off like music or put down like literature – they are there for the enjoyment of the public at large, as users, visitors or just passers-by. It is high time we started giving our towns and cities back to people.

It is not part of my argument that we should ignore the needs of modern living or the economic advantages that may be conferred by new development. What I do believe is that planning applications should be refused over and over again until a result is secured which will make a demonstrable and positive contribution to the quality of the built urban environment and the quality of life to be enjoyed by the people who use it. We should not be bullied by developers, even where a town or city is desperate for development. Let the poor and insensitive ones go away in frustration and bad grace and let them go out of business. There are, fortunately, always a few developers with a much more sensitive and caring approach to the places in which they operate. They will be helped to stay in business if they do good

work. We are the consumers. Our views are sovereign.

Similarly, unless something fairly radical is done about traffic in our towns and cities – particularly the unchecked reliance on private cars – our town centres and city centres are, quite simply, going to die.

Many town centres are a mess because there is nobody who cares about them as a whole. They suffer from organizational neglect. In some places Town Centre Managers have been successfully introduced to cut through the diffused, uncoordinated control exercised by existing local authority departments. They have a janitorial role (similar to the Manager of a Shopping Centre); a responsibility for promoting and developing the town centre; and, handling day-to-day management. It requires commitment and a low-key, persistent individual with access to decision-makers.

Small initiatives are important, such as moving obstacles on the pavement or cutting down the noise and pollution for those who like to eat outside. Experiment is important. Successful results can be used to assemble a coalition of interests to push worthwhile initiatives in the right direction.

Do not neglect the value of a little 'urban fun' – Terry Farrell's Egyptian-style railway station at East Putney and an ingenious water sculpture over the whole front of a shop in Covent Garden, London – or 'escapism', like these buildings and landscaping dripping exuberantly down the hillside in a Canary Islands tropical tourist paradise.

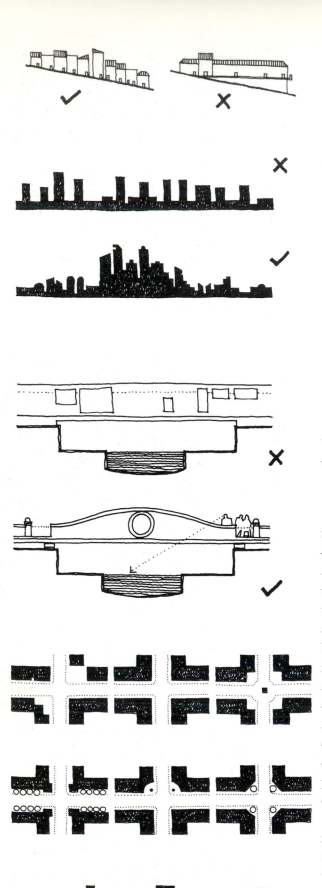

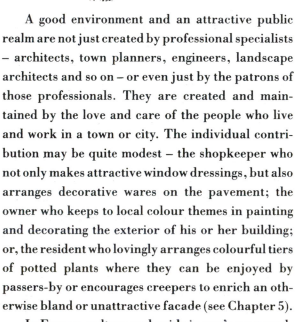

A good environment and an attractive public realm are not just created by professional specialists – architects, town planners, engineers, landscape architects and so on – or even just by the patrons of those professionals. They are created and maintained by the love and care of the people who live and work in a town or city. The individual contribution may be quite modest – the shopkeeper who not only makes attractive window dressings, but also arranges decorative wares on the pavement; the owner who keeps to local colour themes in painting and decorating the exterior of his or her building; or, the resident who lovingly arranges colourful tiers of potted plants where they can be enjoyed by passers-by or encourages creepers to enrich an otherwise bland or unattractive facade (see Chapter 5).

In France, culture and pride in one's surroundings are vote winners. In England, Ministers still regard the same things as vote losers, in the context that the majority of people view decay, litter and urban squalor as someone else's problem. Look how the British Government's own *Time for Design* Initiative and its subsequent monitoring were starved of resources. The *me first* ethos of the so-called Enterprise Culture has contributed to an unhealthy public attitude to such problems. Actually what we urgently need is a renaissance of our once strong civic pride.

Simple rules or principles for the design and management of the public realm can be very effective. Many countries have such codes and these appear not to inhibit the good designer from producing wholly original, modern designs, which are appropriate to the context. It must surely be preferable to have such guidance spelled out at the briefing stage, before the architect has become wedded to a particular solution, than afterwards to subject a design to interference and arbitrary compromise on the basis of the subjective judgements of officials and politicians. Good architects should not fear such guidance which would seek not only to prevent the poor and mediocre but also to encourage excellence and innovation.

A society that lists buildings for preservation, designates conservation areas and selects other areas as being of outstanding natural beauty, is clearly declaring its belief in objective standards
(Lord St John of Fawsley, Foreword to 'Planning for Beauty').

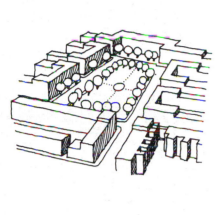

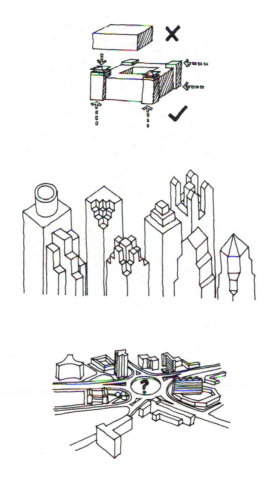

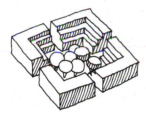

Planning authorities need to draw up local design guidelines and use them sensibly – as a checklist to encourage good design, not as a straightjacket to stifle creativity or original thought. This has been done successfully in other places around the world. The cities of Washington and San Francisco have established height guidelines. Bologna insists on arcades. Lanzarote insists on low rise development in white and dark green. Most United States cities have planning codes which consider the critical variables of use, bulk, height, density, building lines.

San Francisco has been particularly farsighted in stipulating appropriate colours – basically pastel shades – for tall buildings, banning mirror glass and prohibiting the overshadowing of public spaces. Street lines are maintained and tall buildings have proper tops. Commercial developers must contribute, in cash or kind, 1 square foot of open space (public square, arcade, atrium, park or garden) for every 50 square feet of built development – *not* in return for more floorspace, but because, without it, planning permission will not be forthcoming.

It is, perhaps, most sensible that national governments should set down urban design guidelines appropriate for the country as a whole, to be used as a checklist. Local planning authorities should then develop, refine and adapt these to suit local circumstances, having regard to variations of topography, heritage, climate, history and culture, the existing context and local colours, materials and decoration.

What needs to happen to secure the renaissance of the public realm? I have five suggestions.

Firstly, we need greater commitment from national governments – and the responsible environmental Ministers. They need to take a greater interest in the design of the public realm. It is not enough to grumble about litter. Litter is a symptom of decay in a public environment which is being starved both of expenditure and imagination. We are drifting towards an environment of private affluence and public squalor.

It is difficult to legislate for good design. That doesn't mean that we mustn't try. For example, in the United Kingdom, I would like to see the Secretary of State for the Environment promulgate a forceful piece of advice to planning authorities which can be given considerable weight in deciding

Local urban design guide-lines can be devised and are useful, as this selection from London and Birmingham, Melbourne, San Francisco and Lanzarote shows:
…work with the local topography
…design the skyline
…make it obvious when a river or canal is being crossed
…design street frontages and corners
…design shopfronts as part of the whole building
…make enclosed outdoor rooms
…design visual markers into the corners and tops of buildings
…mark the entrances to urban centres
…give tall buildings distinctive profiles, especially the tops
…where important, insist on consistency of scale and colour.

planning and development applications. A suggested text for this is given at the end of this book. As a minimum, design must become a *material consideration* in determining planning applications. The hands-off brigade have failed totally to demonstrate that the public environment is safe in their hands in the absence of planning control and design guidance.

Secondly, some radical changes are needed in the training of the professions concerned with the design of the urban environment – architects, town planners, landscape architects, engineers, surveyors, estate managers and so on. The gaps between them have got to be closed. It is all too often in the Schools that the rot sets in. What is needed is joint training at every opportunity – shared foundation courses, interdisciplinary projects and staff-swapping between departments.

Thirdly, urban design needs to be properly recognized within local planning authority structures. It is more than a tame architect giving, on a part-time basis, design observations on never-ending piles of mediocre planning applications. It is about caring for the physical quality of the area as a whole – looking after its past and designing its future. It is

about making good things happen.

Fourthly, what can the professional institutions do? They should be aiming to draw into the professions people with the right capabilities to improve the urban environment. Design skills are important. But so is a sensitive approach to the after-care and management of places, an understanding of the economic and social dynamics of change and the ability to seize opportunities as they are presented.

Fifthly and finally, community and professionals must always be thinking good design. Good design means added value. It also means caring about the community and their physical environment.

What is required to achieve the vision of towns and cities which are more people-friendly is not head-on confrontation – usually messy and unsuccessful – but, instead, the reinforcement of existing worthwhile initiatives and momentum and the abandonment of the detrimental ones. The trick is, judo-style, to give a good push to everything which is going in the right direction. *At the same time we must stop accepting the mediocre and second best in town design.*

Design must be a material consideration, in both the popular and legal senses of the word, in assessing all proposals for urban development. Designers and developers should be invited to submit short design statements with their proposals. For example, why is the corner of this new Belfast departmental store, in Northern Ireland, curved? Is the entrance clear? Is it the right height and form for this particular street? Are the materials appropriate? Does it provide a pedestrian-friendly frontage? ...and so on. If this book gives encouragement to ask these and other questions about proposals which will change the face of our towns and cities throughout the world, then it will have succeeded in its purpose.

Recommendations/action checklist

To everyone:

1 Look at every proposal again and again. How can it be made better? How does it square up to the axioms in the preceding ten Chapters of this book?

2 We must all care more about the physical environment and believe in good design.

3 We need to foster a more open, collaborative approach amongst all participants in the development process.

4 We need to identify leaders who will look after our towns and cities, encourage the right things to happen and stop the bad things.

To central government:

1 Give greater priority to the physical environment and the long-term future.

2 Promulgate clear design advice in ministerial circulars and policy statements.

To local planning authorities:

1 Recognize the importance of urban design.

2 Appoint appropriate personnel at all levels of seniority to handle urban design tasks.

To the professional institutions:

1 Break down professional demarcations. The environmental professions should all be natural allies, working together for the good of the environment.

2 Encourage, in particular, the training of people with urban design skills.

To the academic institutions:

1 Break down narrow, insular teaching practices.

2 Encourage multi-disciplinary working and studying at staff and student level.

It is easy for everyone to love townscape like this – around Lincoln Cathedral, England. At the end of the day, what matters most is that we try to understand why we like what has succeeded in the past. Such an understanding can, and must, inform the way in which we design and manage new, innovative environments. It will also help us to stem the drift into universal, anonymous mediocrity. Then, once again, perhaps we can create more people-friendly towns and cities.

Postscript
Model Guidelines for Design and Planning Control

The following guidelines are drawn from a text prepared by the author in 1989 for discussion between the Royal Town Planning Institute, the Royal Institute of British Architects, the development industry and the Department of the Environment, United Kingdom. The text was formally submitted to the Secretary of State for the Environment in March 1990 as a suggested basis for a Ministerial Circular or Planning Policy Guidance Note on Design and Planning Control. Such guidelines could form a useful foundation for the drawing up of guidance which is specifically relevant to a particular town, city, region or country. They summarize the principal tenets of this book.

The importance of good design

1 This advice is aimed at improving what is often a difficult area of planning control, to the benefit of those making development proposals, planning authorities and the public. Developers and planning authorities need to recognize the importance of engaging good design skills and striving for high standards of design.

2 Good design is not just socially responsible. It also adds value to development, for example, by commanding good rents, by maintaining enhanced capital growth and by requiring less maintenance. Well-designed development need not be costly – imagination, creativity and sensitivity can create high quality at low or modest cost. Simply cladding a poor design in expensive materials will not achieve this.

3 Good design must be the aim of everyone involved in the development process. The products should be buildings which are well designed for their purpose and their surroundings, and a public environment (the spaces between buildings) which is attractive to use, visually stimulating and easy to manage and maintain.

4 The planning process should seek to encourage and facilitate excellence, innovation and creativity in design while discouraging and preventing poor and mediocre proposals. Design should be a material consideration in the determination of all applications for development.

5 Good design should essentially be the responsibility of the client – as developer, owner, financier or builder – and the designer – as architect, artist or craftsman. This responsibility is not always met – for example, where economic viability obscures most, if not all, design considerations. Nor is it axiomatic that all designers are good designers. It is therefore important that the public, usually through the medium of the planning authority, should develop helpful means of encouraging better design in their areas.

6 Good design is not easy to define, because it is subjective and it depends whose value systems are being applied. It should, however, be possible to reach widespread agreement that the basic aim is to create buildings and spaces which combine to form an attractive public realm – that is, places which can be seen and enjoyed by the public.

7 What is of particular importance is the recognition that good design is not just a matter of attention to elevational design.

Development control

8 Planning authorities should, therefore, con-

sider the design aspect of development proposals in relation both to their intrinsic qualities and to their setting. Such consideration should include:

...the nature of the uses proposed and their impact on their surroundings. Uses at ground level should be appropriate to a pedestrian environment and mixed uses should be encouraged on urban sites wherever practicable.

...the scale, height, bulk and density of the proposed development. These should be appropriate to the specific context. Since buildings are perceived at different distances – on the skyline, down a street or across a square, or close to eye level and people walking about – their visual impact needs to be considered at each of these scales. Roofscape – as an important fifth elevation – should not be neglected.

...the layout of buildings, space about buildings and landscape treatment. Left-over tracts of land should be avoided and generally layouts should aim to produce attractive, intricate places related to the scale of people walking. It will be important to exploit the individuality,

uniqueness and differences between places and to encourage freedom of access and movement, particularly for pedestrians. The needs of the disabled must also be positively taken into account. Good landscaping, whether hard or soft, formal or informal, is important – its mellowing and softening effect helps to knit development together to form an attractive, coherent whole.

...access, roads and parking areas. Access arrangements need to be clear, safe and efficient and designed to minimize harmful impacts by motor vehicles – such as noise, pollution, visual intrusion, severance and danger – upon the local environment.

...the character and quality of the local environment, including the relationship to any adjoining buildings. New development should relate to its physical context in appropriate ways – for example, in scale, use, colour, materials and so on. This does not imply copying of existing styles or pastiche. It should be possible for new buildings to have the same richness, individuality, intricacy and user-friendly qualities as tradi-

tional, well-loved development. Planning control should not stifle experiment, originality or initiative.

9 Planning authorities should make clear their reasons for preferences regarding materials, colours, elevational design and detail and should avoid unnecessary interference in detail design and insistence on trivial alterations. If the overall design concept is well conceived, this will be unnecessary. If it is not, it is unlikely materially to be improved by minor adjustments.

10 Planning permission should be withheld when development proposals have insufficient regard for their impact on neighbouring property or on the local environment, or to the lneeds of access or represent an over-development of the site. In the circumstances of such clear-cut grounds for the refusal of permission, the applicant should at once be invited to submit revised proposals, without having to wait for formal determination.

11 Drawings should illustrate the proposals in their context, using perspectives, photo-mon-

tages or other three-dimensional presentation techniques whenever appropriate. Applicants must demonstrate that they have properly addressed the five sets of design considerations set out above, in the context of any additional specific guidance for the area or site issued by the planning authority. Provided this has satisfactorily been done and there are no other planning objections, permission should always be forthcoming.

12 Many planning applications are for relatively small-scale proposals such as extensions, conversions and minor buildings – often, though not always, submitted by applicants other than architects – which do little to enhance the local environment and whose cumulative effect can be very detrimental to local amenity. In these cases planning authorities should have a positive role in fostering better standards and awareness of the benefits of good design to the owner or developer.

Heritage areas

13 Many planning regimes provide for additional control in historic or conservation areas. These powers are aimed at the need to preserve and enhance the character or appearance of an area. This should not preclude the possibility of new development taking place in such areas, provided that it is designed in a sensitive manner, having regard to the special character of the area in question.

14 In historic or conservation areas, in addition to the considerations set out above, it is particularly important that new development should harmonize with the existing townscape, materials, historical features and local vernacular style. Innovative, sensitive design will usually be preferred to a pastiche replication of historical styles, providing it is sympathetic and appropriate to its surroundings.

Statutory plans

15 Planning authorities should give clearly expressed, objective design advice which is appropriate to their area. General principles should be contained, as far as practicable, in adopted statutory plans. These might, for example, include:

…the definition of areas in which mixed uses will be encouraged to create variety and a lively, safe environment;

…general height guidelines for development (either as figured dimensions or numbers of storeys) – with exceptions for buildings which, by virtue of their use or form, make a positive contribution to the skyline as landmarks;

…the encouragement of good craftsmanship, landscaping and the integration of pieces of art to enrich the public environment;

…the need to make development permeable (easy to move through and around) and legible (easy to understand and recognize where you are);

…the desirability for buildings, where appropriate, to be robust (able to adapt over time to changing opportunities and needs);

…the desirability of choosing materials for their permanence, durability, mellowing and enduring qualities, and for ease of maintenance;

…the desirability of avoiding wholesale rapid

change, by encouraging the development of smaller sites, setting limits on the extent of site assembly or breaking up larger sites into more easily managed components of incremental development;

...the encouragement of more sensitive, friendly development in which colour, pattern, decoration, texture and materials – as well as technical excellence and innovation – combine to create enjoyable buildings and development; and

...the need for people to have a say in the design of the physical environment in which they live, work, shop and play.

Site briefs

16 In addition, planning authorities should prepare planning briefs or design briefs for sites which are important, environmentally sensitive or difficult to develop. These can be used not only to summarize the relevant policies in local plans, but also to provide essential information and design objectives related to the specific site, such as height guidance, views or view corridors to be maintained, uses, materials, roof profile or skyline, grain of development, pedestrian routes and so on.

Consultation

17 Applicants should always consult the planning authority before formulating a development proposal to ensure that they have a clear understanding of the authority's objectives and the policies and principles against which the development proposal will subsequently be judged.

Afterword by Kevin Murray

This book is undoubtedly a seminal piece whose message is being constantly validated over time. Although partly inspired by Francis' reaction against the qualities of alienating corporate urbanism which he witnessed emerging during the 1980s, it is the important observations and exhortations about synthesis – or 'closing the gaps', as he sometimes called it – which distinguish it from other, narrower works on design, planning, or urbanism. In many ways, by seeking to place urban design at the centre of a vision for a better quality of urban living, he was both of his time and ahead of his time.

Although Francis was passionate about towns and cities he did not simply wax lyrically about those places he liked. He wanted to turn his experience and insights – extensive in both time and space – into something which has practical value for professionals, politicians, communities, developers and investors. His analysis and recommendations are relevant today and will surely remain so for some time to come. This is why the book needs to be read and re-read by a wide range of new audiences over time.

Francis believed that urban design was a critical philosophy and discipline because places matter more than the individual components which make them up – buildings, spaces and structures. Fundamentally, the austere design simplicity of the modernist era of planning failed to create the enduring places people want and need. A new – or arguably, traditional – integrative approach to placemaking was required.

Although there is still a prevalent object fetishism in architecture and public art, the holistic urban design approach has continued to gain ground, not least on mainland Europe where it never really disappeared. It has been at the forefront of the much admired renaissance of post Franco Barcelona, not only in modest neighbourhood spaces but in the philosophy behind the Olympic Village. Other approaches have been pursued across the Netherlands and in the dramatic reconstruction of Berlin since re-unification.

Francis would be moderately impressed to find that urban design has slowly crept into the mainstream of UK planning and regeneration during the 1990s, featuring both in government guidance – which he pressed for strongly – and in the personal initiatives of John Gummer, when a minister.

Regeneration projects such as Newcastle Quayside, Birmingham's Brindley Place, and more recently the post-bomb reconstruction of central Manchester, all exhibit the stronger sense of integrated urban design which has sought to emulate their international counterparts. On housing led development too, a distinctive neighbourhood approach has been pioneered by projects as diverse as Hulme in Manchester, Crown Street in Glasgow and the Duchy of Cornwall development at Poundbury, Dorchester. Some of these draw from the American approach of 'new urbanism' with its strong principles and building codes framed to challenge the placelessness of strips, malls and suburban sprawl. Francis' former practice sought to apply these in their plan for the urban village of West Silvertown in London's Royal Docks.

Perhaps one of the biggest steps in the UK has been the strong recommendation in Lord Rogers' Urban Task Force Report that urban design – particularly three-dimensional spatial master planning – should play a key part in the regeneration of towns, cities and their neighbourhoods. Francis undoubtedly supported this objective – which he enjoyed undertaking himself – but would probably have settled for a less overtly 'architectural' approach than the Task Force report promotes.

The need for appropriate multi-disciplinary skills, training and practice was identified as crucial by Francis more than a decade before the Task Force, but with negligible follow through. A committed architect-planner, he was concerned that his was a dying breed, with architects acting primarily in the interests of individual developer clients, while planners focused on sectoral policies and processes.

The 'joined up thinking' which latterly became the watchword of political protagonists such as John Prescott, was trailed in Francis' RTPI Presidential theme during 1988. He would have been delighted at the formation of the multi-professional Urban Design Alliance, following on his own founding of the Urban Design Group some 20 years earlier. However, the Alliance has a long way to go to make a telling impact on the training of its constituent professionals and on the environments they create. Nevertheless UDAL has made a positive impact in a number of areas, including widening the scope of the successor to the Royal Fine Arts Commission to become the Commission for Architecture *and* the Built Environment. As a supporter of many of the developments which Stuart Lipton undertook – he would be urging us to watch the progress of CABE with interest.

Francis considered that narrow professionalism was at the root of many townscape problems and he was not afraid to become unpopular by charging fellow architects and planners, not to mention surveyors and engineers, with this crime. Nowhere was he more concerned about the gaps than in the design, implementation and management of the public realm. He would surely be impressed at the progress made in European cities such as Copenhagen, Prague and Munich in developing an attractive network of people-friendly streets and spaces. These have been matched in their own way by progressive improvements in central UK cities such as Birmingham, Manchester, Glasgow and Cambridge.

Despite this progress many American cities retain a strong preference for vehicular access and dominance of town centres. There seems to be a general unwillingness to adopt the progressive removal of vehicles pioneered by Copenhagen over a thirty-year period. Nevertheless impressive steps have been made in Portland, Oregon, where a highway has been removed to create a new riverfront park; and San Francisco, where innovative public realm improvements are emerging along the corridors of elevated highways irreparably damaged by earthquake. Even New York's sidewalks and public spaces have been improved dramatically over a decade which has seen Manhatten become cleaner, safer and more convivial for residents and visitors alike.

As Francis' drawings in this book testify, he was a lover of variety, vitality and the richness of the urban scene. Drawing on the influential work of Jane Jacobs he was a passionate believer in the need for mixed use. This philosophy has clearly moved forward since the book was first published, gradually shifting towards the mainstream of a number of planning regimes across the globe. In the UK this has been stimulated by the advocacy of the Urban Villages Group, research by a range of bodies, and advocacy in government guidance. Some successes have been achieved in locations such as Birmingham's Jewellery Quarter, Newcastle's Grainger Town and Edinburgh's historic port area of Leith. Specific area strategies have been adopted in Sheffield, Belfast and Dublin, focusing on both the production and consumption of cultural industries.

The mixed use challenge is to secure enough interest to stimulate regeneration through human biodiversity, although there is always the danger of adverse impacts working against the intrinsic qualities which laid the foundations of success. One-time favourites of Francis, such as London's Covent Garden and Dublin's Temple Bar, now exhibit some of those problematic qualities. Perhaps they need some constraints on the level of commercial occupancy, as are applied in New York's SoHo to protect the role of its artistic and creative communities.

Francis identified our love affair with the motor car as a long-term problem for the health of our cities and, more importantly, for global sustainability. While the problems have worsened in many areas over recent years there have been improvements too. I believe he would have welcomed Croydon's new Tramlink in South London, which would have taken him from his Beckenham home to the Croydon Library, one of his most satisfying development projects. New public transit systems in Manchester, Grenoble, Portland and Sydney have all given new dimensions to those cities. Hopefully the Heathrow Express and New Jubilee Line would have mitigated Francis' frequent criticisms of the shortcomings of the London transport system.

It is clear therefore that in many of the areas of urban design which were of great concern to Francis Tibbalds, some positive progress has been made. Francis would undoubtedly accept those, but he would not rest on any laurels. We have not gone nearly far enough. He would look to move the debate forward, spreading the word to new audiences, using different arguments. He might contend that:

1 Good urban design is crucial to the local economy, both in terms of attracting and holding residents and workers. In the globalised, footloose economy of the information age, the comparative attractiveness of places is also important in retaining expenditure and taxation locally.

2 Tourism is positively shaped by good urban design. Those with choice will tend to visit attractive places, whether historic or modern. Ironically, the once mocked Disney Corporation are now becoming leading exponents of urban design in creating successful new settlements.

3 Our objectives of sustainable development can be assisted by good urban design which stimulates reinvestment in the existing urban fabric, rather than wasteful exploitation of virgin land.

4 Most of all, I believe, Francis would argue that good urban design, the very nurturing of our towns and cities – is the responsibility of all of us, whether professionals, politicians, developers or members of the public.

If those of us who have the opportunity can take forward Francis Tibbalds' urban design vision with even half of his passion, then together we can make a difference by creating successful places for real people.

Kevin Murray
April 2000

Bibliography

Bibliography

This is not intended to be a comprehensive bibliography of books about urban design. Rather it is a compilation of source material and a number of other works which have been influential in the preparation of this book.

The Ascent of Man by J. Bronowski; British Broadcasting Corporation, 1973. The book of the outstanding television documentary, which charted in a most expansive manner the rise of mankind as shapers of our environment and future.

Beazley's Design and Detail of the Space between Buildings by Angi Pinder and Alan Pinder; E. & F.N. Spon, 1990. A new edition of a book which has, for many years, been an invaluable guide to hard landscape design.

City Centre Design Strategy by Tibbalds Colbourne Karski Williams Monro; City of Birmingham, 1990. Part of a series of urban design studies commissioned by the city, taking a robust, coherent, apolitical vision over a thirty/forty year time span, of ways of improving the central area of Birmingham as opportunities for change occur.

A City is not a Tree by Christopher Alexander; *Architectural Forum*, 1965 and *Design* 1966. This article, which was selected for one of the 1965 Kaufmann International Design Awards, is one of the most influential ever written about city planning. In a mere nine pages, Dr Alexander – a mathematician as well as an architectural scholar – cogently argues that a natural city has the organization of a 'semi-lattice', but when we organize a city artificially, we make the mistake of doing it in a hierarchical fashion, like a tree.

The Death and Life of Great American Cities by Jane Jacobs; Random House Inc., 1961. The book that cogently challenged hitherto fashionable theories of urban planning and land use zoning.

Green Paper on the Urban Environment. Commission of the European Communities; Brussels, June 1990. A welcome synoptic overview of problems of the urban environment in their widest sense, demonstrating that to reach solutions, traditional sectoral boundaries need to be crossed.

How Do You Want to Live? A Report on the Human Habitat for the Department of the Environment; HMSO, 1972. A study of public opinion, undertaken at the request of the then Secretary of State for the Environment, The Rt Hon. Peter Walker MP, in connection with the United Nations Conference on the Human Environment, Stockholm, June 1972.

Living over the Shop – A Guide to the Provision of Housing above Shops in Town Centres; NHTPC, June 1990. A first Report of a two year Project set up by Ann Petherick and sponsored by the Joseph Rowntree Foundation.

Marvellous Melbourne 2000 – An Overview of Planning Opportunities with International Comparisons by Francis Tibbalds/Tibbalds Colbourne Karski Williams Monro; Department of Planning and Urban Growth, State of Victoria, Australia; July 1990. A Study for the Minister of Planning and Urban Growth aimed at identifying, considering and recommending, against a wide international perspective, opportunities for the enhancement of Central Melbourne as an international city.

Our Approach to Making User-Friendly Environments: 14 Principles of Good Practice by Tibbalds Colbourne Karski Williams Monro, London 1990. A set of principles, continually being refined, which is being used to guide projects and design work and as a management tool for staff training.

Planning for Beauty – The Case for Design Guidelines by Judy Hillman; Royal Fine Art Commission, HMSO, April 1990. A useful guide through what has become a real minefield – the relationship between design control and planning control.

The Public vs The Private Realm – the Implications for Urban Design of the Decline of the Public Realm by Francis Tibbalds; AJ Urban Design series; *The Architects Journal*, 7.11.90. A contribution to a series of three issues of the AJ on urban design, running from October 24 1990.

Responsive Environments – A Manual for Designers by Bentley Alcock Murrain McGlynn Smith; The Architectural Press, 1985. One of the first really comprehensive books to look at making places more 'user friendly' in terms of how they are used, understood and personalized.

Shahestan Pahlavi – A New City Centre for Tehran – Book Two: *The Urban Design*; Llewelyn-Davies International, 1976. The author was Principal Architect Planner on the team and wrote the majority of the text of this volume, dealing with urban design proposals for the new centre.

Townscape by Gordon Cullen; The *Architectural Press* 1961. Gordon Cullen's robust concepts of serial vision, place and content are still directly relevant today. The sketches remain wonderful too.

Traffic in Towns – A Study of the Long Term Problems of Traffic in Urban Areas; Report of the Steering Group and Working Group appointed by the Minister of Transport; HMSO 1963. Commonly known as The Buchanan Report, this was the first real analysis of the relationship between accessibility, environmental quality and investment. It coined the now widely accepted notions of defining for each street an 'environmental capacity' and the definition of 'environmental areas' from which 'extraneous traffic' should be strictly excluded. It was, and still is, a landmark study.

Traffic Calming – Through Integrated Urban Planning by H.G. Vahl and J. Gisks; Editions Amarcande, December 1989. A useful primer, available in four languages, by two Dutch municipal engineers, funded by the Volvo Traffic Safety Award 1986, sharing considerable technical know-how and illustrating this with examples from the Netherlands and France.

Transport in Cities by Brian Richards; Architecture Design and Technology Press, 1990. This book succeeds *New Movement in Cities* [1966] and *Moving in Cities* [1976] by the same author and cogently demonstrates that there are viable and proven alternatives to the present nightmare of traffic congestion and pollution.

Urban Design – a special issue of *The Planner*; Journal of the Royal Town Planning Institute; March 1988. This issue helped reveal a strong latent interest in the subject of urban design amongst the British planning profession.

A Vision of Britain – a Personal View of Architecture by His Royal Highness the Prince of Wales; Doubleday, 1989. The book of the landmark television documentary in which Prince Charles not only dramatically raised public interest in the design of the built environment, but also cogently challenged '*the fashionable theories of a professional establishment which has made the layman feel he has no legitimate opinions*'.

Index